Chevrolet TPI &
Engine Swapping

Written by

Mike Knell

Edited by

ERIC HEINITZ

&

JON-MANJI

Published & Distributed by

J.T.R.

P.O. Box 66 • Livermore, CA 94551

Fourth Edition… October 1993

Printed in the United States of America

Disclaimer of Warranties

The information contained in this manual is based upon the latest data available at the time of publication and has been obtained and compiled from various sources believed to be reliable. However, the possibility exists that some manufacturers made changes that could not be included in this manual. While every attempt has been made to provide accurate information and because the quality of parts, materials and methods are beyond our control, no responsibility is assumed by the publisher or anyone connected with it for loss or damages suffered through reliance on or reference to any information contained in this publication.

TABLE OF CONTENTS

FOREWORD

If you plan on doing an engine swap, you should ask yourself the following questions:

1. Can you afford the swap? Swaps normally cost a lot of money.

2. Do you have the experience, equipment, and facilities to do the swap? Swaps often require special tools and lots of room.

3. Do you have the time to do the swap? Swaps normally take a lot of time.

4. Most importantly, do you have the enthusiasm to complete the swap? We have seen many people spend a lot of time and money trying to do an engine swap, only to lose their enthusiasm, and give up on the swap.

The purpose of this manual is to show how to install Chevrolet fuel-injected engines into cars and trucks that were not originally equipped with fuel-injected engines. It shows examples of vehicles with *engine swaps* such as the Jaguar, S-10 Truck, Volvo, and even the Chevrolet V8 into the 1984 Ford Mustang SVO. This is to illustrate the adaptability of the fuel-injected engines, and show that wiring, cooling, fuel systems, exhaust, and air conditioning all work on the same basic principles.

This manual is not intended to replace the factory shop manuals for your engine and your vehicle (That's right, two more manuals!), but to provide supplemental information for your engine change. The Helm service manuals (not Haynes, not Chiltons, not Mitchells, but Helm) provide the best information for wiring information, repairs, and diagnostics. These are the same books that Chevrolet Dealerships use. Helm's phone number is (800)782-4356, they accept credit card orders for your convenience.

This manual will help guide you through your engine swap, or stop you from getting into a project that you won't be able to complete.

The vehicles in this manual are intended to be daily drivers, and are smog legal according to California smog laws, unless otherwise noted. JTR has always believed in smog legal engine swaps, because it makes the vehicle easier to own and register. It also makes the vehicle more valuable.

IMPORTANT!

Most people are under the impression that if they buy a fuel-injection system, they can simply bolt it onto their engine, and drive off with more power and better fuel economy. Needless to say, these people are in for a big lesson: Fuel-injection by itself will improve drivability, but it will not make a slow engine fast, or make a gas guzzler into an economy car. The real reason for the power is the engine long-block. If you want power, put your money in the long-block.

INTRODUCTION

WARNINGS

Engine Swaps are not for "average shade tree mechanics"!

The original intention of this manual was to make it possible for "average shade tree mechanics" to install TPI (Tuned Port Injection) and TBI (Throttle Body Injection) engines into older cars and trucks. However, after testing the manual on several "average shade tree mechanics" and observing their swaps, we learned that they could often make the engines run, but made numerous mistakes in wiring, fuel systems, hose routing, hose selection, cooling, exhaust, emission control equipment, air conditioning — just about everything imaginable. A lot of the mistakes could have been dangerous. In other words, the "average shade tree mechanic" was not qualified to do the TPI or TBI engine swap, or any engine swap.

Engine swaps require experience, knowledge, patience, and a willingness to look things up in a book or shop manual. From these experiences, we can only advise most people not to do TPI or TBI engine swaps unless they are experienced mechanics, or have experienced mechanics who will carefully inspect the conversion before the vehicle is started, and again before the vehicle is driven.

Remember, the purpose of an engine swap is to make the vehicle better, and if you can not make it better, it is not worth doing.

COST AND TIME

After someone has *successfully* completed an engine swap, we ask the question, "Was it as much work as you expected?"

The usual answer is, "the engine swap was a lot more work than I expected, but I could do it in half as much time if I did it again."

As for cost, most people say the complete conversion cost about twice as much as originally planned.

TIME AND EXPERIENCE

It took over four years to complete this manual. A large part of that time involved assisting and observing people with their engine conversions. We would not actually do other people's conversions, but we would guide them if they were doing something wrong or dangerous. In a sense, we acted as consultants.

On the other hand, we have performed a number of engine swaps on our own vehicles, which are used as daily drivers and some are shown in this manual. We know how to do engine swaps, but we always learn something new from other people's engine swaps. We mention this because almost every engine swap presents challenges[1] that take more time and money than originally expected.

1.Difficulties, problems.

INTRODUCTION

FRUSTRATION FACTORS

Back to engine swaps. The most common denominator of all the conversion problems boiled down to **FRUSTRATION**. Invariably, some things do not go as planned. Mostly, people got frustrated with the amount of time required to complete the conversion. Often, special order parts are required with an engine swap. Invariably, this means a one or two week wait. Even after the vehicle is running, it may seem like it is never finished—wires may need to be tucked away and hidden, the air conditioning hoses may not be hooked up, the car may overheat, an alternator can fail.

Other people got frustrated by the cost of the conversion. Most people had no idea how much the completed conversion would cost. A lot of people had to stop working on their conversions because they ran out of money: Electric fuel pumps, air cleaner ducting, driveshaft modifications, air conditioning hoses, power steering hoses, throttle cables, motor mounts, and exhaust work, can literally cost thousands of dollars on some conversions. That's right, thousands of dollars!

Please read this manual and take notes of the cost and time required so that if you decide to do an engine swap, you will not get *too* frustrated.

IT'S WORTH THE WORK

On a more positive note, the late model fuel-injected engines have great reliability, drivability, and serviceability. We find the fuel-injected engines to be far superior to carbureted engines. With equal amounts of experience, the fuel-injected engines are easier to diagnose for problems than carbureted engines: The engine's trouble codes are easily accessed, and the factory shop manuals (available from Helm) have trouble shooting charts that make diagnosing problems straightforward and accurate.

BUT IT NEEDS OVERDRIVE!

Some people have greatly exaggerated the advantages of fuel-injection in terms of power gains and fuel economy. The truly significant fuel economy gains of fuel-injection are only realized with overdrive transmissions and tall gear ratios. To put it another way, powerful engines can get good gas mileage when used with overdrive transmissions and tall gearing. It's the ability of fuel-injection to provide the proper fuel/air ratio when the engine is under load at low engine speeds, that fuel-injection really stands apart from carburetors.

The other tangible advantages of fuel-injection are its consistent drivability during different weather conditions, and at different altitudes. The TPI/TBI engines always run good. And they always start well.

MORE WARNINGS

The swaps shown in this manual were either done by ourselves for ourselves, or by hard-core gearheads who did the conversions for themselves.

The best conversions we have seen are those performed by the owners of the vehicles, because they cared about what they were doing and took the time and spent the money to do things right without cutting corners.

The people who cut corners almost always end up spending more money trying to fix their mistakes than the people who do their conversions correctly the first time. An example is when the person does not spend enough money on the cooling system, and he has to replace the engine because he overheated it.

INTRODUCTION

ENGINE SWAPS: IT'S MORE THAN MOTOR MOUNTS

When *most* people look at engine swaps, they usually look at the motor mounts. The motor mounts are a very small part of an engine swap. They are important, but nearly anybody can make a set of motor mounts for their particular engine swap. The *experienced* engine swappers look at oil pan clearance, steering clearance, exhaust clearance, fan clearance, hood clearance, ground clearance, firewall clearance, speedometer cable clearance and transmission tunnel clearance. The *experienced* swappers look at power steering hoses, shift linkage, clutch linkage, throttle linkage, wire routing, air conditioning hoses, radiator hoses, radiators, cooling fans, exhaust systems, fuel systems, and whatever else is required for the engine swap.

ENGINE SWAPS: THEY TAKE TIME

We are often asked if we do "turn-key" conversions, or if we know of a shop that will do a complete engine swap for their vehicle.

The answer is, "no," and, "no."

Most shops in our area have to charge $50/hour to stay in business. A typical Jaguar TPI V8 engine swap takes about 100 hours. The labor cost alone will be $5,000. Most people walk away from those price quotes.

We often hear of shops that take on TPI engine swaps for Jaguars, Datsun Z cars, Chevrolet S-10 trucks, and even Volvos, yet we rarely see a *finished* conversion leaving the shop. Invariably, the conversion turns out to be more involved than the shop expected, and the project gets put on the back burner... for a long time.

This manual is for the do-it-yourselfer who enjoys working on his or her own vehicle. If you have a shop, this manual is to warn you about doing TPI engine swaps for customers.

RECOMMENDED READING:

How to Repair and Modify Chevrolet Fuel Injection (Classic Motorbooks part #115879ap $19.95, phone (800)826-6600). This book explains in layman's terms, how to do basic work on TPI and TBI engines with basic shop tools.

INTRODUCTION

RECYCLING AND ENVIRONMENTAL CONCERNS

The main purpose of most engine swaps is for improved performance. With environmental concerns becoming increasingly important, we do most of our conversions with the goal to reduce emissions and improve fuel economy, as well as improve performance. This world has limited resources and the effects of pollution and fuel shortages have made themselves known with dirty air and high fuel prices.

By using engines and transmissions from wrecking yards, we recycle used parts. By using overdrive transmissions and the late model fuel-injected engines, the fuel economy and emissions levels of many V8 converted vehicles is improved compared to the original engines and transmissions.

Our V8 powered Jaguar XJ-S averages about 18 mpg, compared to 12 mpg with the original V-12 engine, and performance is much better. The overdrive transmission is greatly responsible for the fuel mileage increase.

Our 305 TBI V8 powered S-10 Blazer gets the same average fuel mileage as it did with the stock, throttle-body-injected 2.8 V6, but the rear axle ratio had to be changed from 3.73 to 3.08 to get the results. Still, the performance is much better than with the original engine. The gear ratio change was responsible for the excellent gas mileage with the more powerful engine.

Our 1981 Malibu Wagon averaged 18 mpg with the original 3.8 V6, three-speed automatic transmission and 2.73 gears. With a 1990 305 TPI/700-R4 overdrive transmission, and the 2.73 gears, the average fuel mileage is 20 mpg, and the freeway mileage is about 24 mpg at 65 mph. The overdrive transmission is greatly responsible for the improved fuel mileage.

The common factor in the above examples is that *reduced engine speed improves fuel economy*. We feel this is so important that it will be emphasized throughout the manual. While it is true that the fuel-injection by itself may improve fuel mileage slightly, the real benefit of fuel-injection is its ability to make an engine run good at low speeds while under load. When fuel-injection is combined with overdrive transmissions and appropriate gearing, performance and economy can be improved way beyond that of a carbureted engine.

A GOOD ENGINE SWAP CAN SAVE MONEY

Although a good engine swap costs a lot of money, the savings (compared to purchasing a new car), are well beyond just the purchase price of a new car. New car prices are in the $10,000 to $25,000 for normal cars. In California, sales tax on a new or used car is 8.25% of the purchase price, registration costs are set as X percent of the "market value" of the car, and then there is the cost of insurance on a new car. As expensive as the engine swaps were on our Chevrolet Wagon, Volvos, Jaguars, and S-10 Trucks, the cost of the conversions were easily justified when compared to the *real costs* of purchasing a newer car.

1982 JAGUAR XJ-6 WITH 1988 CAMARO 350 TPI/700-R4 TRANSMISSION

This is the engine compartment of the first TPI installation we had ever done. To be honest, the TPI engine scared us. It took us over two months to complete the conversion. A "normal" carbureted V8 conversion would have taken about two weeks. Most of the extra time consisted of waiting for special order parts and figuring out a couple of details concerning the Jaguar electric speedometer and the Chevrolet vehicle speed sensor and how to tie them together. The cooling system and air cleaner ducting required more work than a carbureted V8 engine swap.

We can now install a Camaro TPI engine into a Jaguar in about three weeks, and it would look better.

The original Jaguar 4.2 liter six-cylinder engine and three-speed automatic transmission averaged about 14 mpg. Now the car averages about 16 mpg and is a lot more powerful. The overdrive transmission is greatly responsible for the improved gas mileage. The car has 2.88 rear end gears, and with the .70 overdrive ratio, the engine turns 1500 rpm at 60 mph. At a steady 65 mph, the car will get 24 mpg.

We were so impressed with the drivability, smoothness and fuel mileage of this fuel-injected drivetrain that we no longer install carbureted engines into our own daily driven vehicles.

1978 JAGUAR XJ-12 RECEIVING 1986 CORVETTE TPI ENGINE

This Jaguar already had a non-smog-legal carbureted Chevrolet 350 V8 and Turbo 400 transmission. The owner decided a fuel-injected engine would offer better performance and drivability, and be smog legal. The owner had no idea that the changeover would require so much time and money. He originally estimated he could complete the conversion in one week, working on the weekend, and after work on the weekdays. Needless to say, the conversion took over twice as long as originally estimated, and cost a lot more than originally figured. Still, two weeks is extremely quick for a first-time TPI engine swap.

This shows the proper way to do an engine swap: With friends and neighbors hanging around with their hands in their pockets making fun of the owner who is in the engine compartment. Notice the proper equipment for an engine swap: Engine hoist, guard dog, and a big hammer.

The exhaust headers are a gray area as far as being smog legal for this swap, but because 1986 Corvettes use tubular headers (which won't fit the Jaguar chassis) and the headers closely approximate the stock Corvette headers, the referee station allowed them. The referee station uses a common-sense approach to many engine swaps: This is a 1978 vehicle, and the engine is a 1986, so the conversion is an upgrade as far as smog laws are concerned.

This conversion differs from the Jaguar shown on page 1–5. The most noticeable differences are the air cleaner and ducting. There are numerous other differences because this is a Corvette engine, not a Camaro engine.

The chapter on engines shows some of the differences between Corvette and Camaro TBI engines, and why it is often better to start with a Camaro engine for most engine swaps.

Note: The gentleman in the engine compartment (opposite page) built the Jaguar for his wife, but he made a common mistake—he did not fully finish (and debug) the conversion before she began driving it.

He did not charge the air conditioner, the engine stalled occasionally because of a bad idle air control (IAC) valve (a $70 part), and the speedometer did not work all the time (see page 5–6).

The results of this mistake: even after he had finished and debugged the conversion, she does not trust the car, and believes she should get a new car—which is what he was trying to avoid when he decided to do the conversion.

1985 VOLVO 760 SEDAN WITH 305 TBI/700-R4 FROM 1991 CAMARO

This car was originally powered by a six-cylinder turbo-diesel which suffered from a rod knock. The cost of a turbo-diesel long block was quite expensive (over $5000), so the owner purchased the low mileage Chevrolet V8 for considerably less than the cost of another Volvo turbo-dudsel engine.

The owner, although skilled mechanically and electrically, had no idea of what he was getting into. Call it dumb luck, but the engine and transmission fit into the car like they were made for each other. The engine position was dictated by the exhaust manifolds. As far as engine swaps go, this was relatively easy. For example:

1. The original turbo-diesel radiator works perfectly with the V8 engine. The fan shroud is a slightly modified 4-cylinder Camaro fan shroud.

2. The air conditioning hoses from the Camaro engine fit the Volvo with only one new hose coupling being required to connect the high side from the compressor to the condenser hose.

3. The 760 Volvo uses an electric speedometer which gets its signal from a sensor mounted in the rear axle assembly, so no speedometer work was required.

4. Diesel engines do not have an ignition system, which is what most tachometers are connected to. The Volvo's Turbo-diesel tachometer works off the Volvo's alternator. The Camaro's alternator has a tachometer connection, and provided the proper signal to drive the Volvo tachometer.

5. The Volvo power steering hoses bolted to the Camaro power steering pump (Volvo uses GM power steering pumps).

6. The Volvo drive shaft uses the same size U-joints as Chevrolets, so the drive shaft only required shortening, and the proper Chevrolet transmission yoke.

7. The Turbo-diesel comes with a fairly big exhaust system, so only new headpipes and a catalytic converter were required.

8. The weight of the V8 was only about 100 lbs heavier than the turtle-diesel, so no suspension modifications were required.

As easy as this conversion sounds, it was a lot of work, and it took a long time to work out all the details such as:

1. Transmission shift linkage

2. Electrical

3. Motor mounts and transmission mounts

4. Fuel system (emissions canister, pumps, fuel tank fittings)

With the stock gears (3.91) and fairly short tires, this car only got about 14 mpg. This low fuel mileage is also because the car is used mostly in city driving. Switching to 3.31 gears (the tallest offered by Volvo for the 760 series) raised the average mileage to 17 mpg. Still, the car is smooth, quiet, and it will blow the doors off of a 760 Turbo Gas Volvo. At the time of this writing, the car has about 20,000 miles on the engine swap.

IT MAY BE UGLY, BUT IT'S A GOOD CAR!

This is the ultimate sleeper—a 1983 Volvo 760 GLE Turbo Diesel with a 1987 350 TPI and a Corvette six-speed transmission and a NOS® nitrous oxide kit. Call it one-upmanship, but after seeing the Volvo that is shown on the previous page, we just had to do a V8 Volvo. In the sleeper theme, it had to be indistinguishable from a stock Volvo. It had to be quiet, it had to look stock, and it had to feel stock. Besides, we already saw one Volvo V8 conversion and it looked pretty easy.

Compared to the Volvo shown on the previous page, the engine is positioned lower and more rearward, mostly so the shifter of the ZF transmission comes out of the stock Volvo console. The transmission tunnel required substantial modifications to accommodate the six-speed. The engine was also offset to the passenger's side about 1-1/4" for the shifter position. The engine position also made room for a quiet engine-driven clutch-fan. The Volvo air cleaner has a large filter, receives cold air from the fender area, and it is quiet. The ducting was custom-made to clear the engine-driven fan. The fan shroud is from a 260 series Volvo.

The engine is completely 1987 Camaro, except for the thermostat housing (from a 1988 Camaro TBI engine), the hose routing, and the passenger's side exhaust manifold (which was replaced with a "rams horn" or "center dump" manifold that is used on 1968–1981 Corvettes). The engine position required changing the exhaust manifold, and this required new spark plug wires.

The accessories on the 1987 engine required radiator modifications, which were not required with the accessories on the 1988–1992 Camaro engine shown on the previous page.

INTRODUCTION

The undercoating above the exhaust system had to be removed and replaced with heat shielding, because of the heat produced by the catalytic converter and the hotter exhaust system (diesels do not come with catalytic converters).

Diesel Volvos use a cable for the clutch release, so the clutch master cylinder and clutch pedal from a Turbo-gas Volvo were used for the hydraulic clutch release, but the 3/4" bore diameter made for a stiff clutch. A .70" diameter clutch master cylinder from Tilton Engineering was then installed for reduced effort and improved feel. In addition, the pivot point of the clutch pedal was modified to reduce effort.

A 3" single exhaust system was installed using a Walker Dynomax muffler (the same muffler used on the GMC Typhoons), but the Volvo sounded like an IROC Camaro. Most people liked the sound, but for the ultimate sleeper, it was not quiet enough, We considered installing a 2-1/2" exhaust system, but did not want to restrict the power of our "sleeper". A Walker 3" Ultra Flo muffler was then added to the exhaust system. The Ultra Flo was the only 3" muffler we could find to fit the Volvo configuration. It is a straight-through design and we did not expect much improvement. It actually dropped the noise level by 4–8 decibels from idle to 4000 rpm—we were extremely pleased. After the second muffler was added, the "normal" noises of the ZF six-speed became noticeable at low speeds.

Because of the potential to over-rev the engine, an MSD rev limiter was installed. We have the rev limiter set at 4800 rpm. Peak horsepower of the stock 350 TPI is at a relatively low 4200 rpm according to published figures, and was verified by using a Vericom 2000 Performance Computer (an on board accelerometer that functions like a fifth wheel). Best quarter mile times are acheived by shifting at about 4600 rpm. People who test drive this car are almost always running into the rev limiter, which is proof that every high-performance car should have a rev limiter installed, especially if other people drive the car.

We originally figured the conversion would take two weeks to complete. It took two weeks just to figure out how to get the six-speed transmission's shifter to come out of the Volvo's shifter hole. It took an additional four weeks to get the car running, and at the time of this writing, the car is still not completely finished (although it has been driven over 14,000 miles).

One point of this discussion is to show how two apparently similar conversions can vary so much. Another point is that there is a big difference between the "perceived" amount of work to do the conversion and the "actual" amount of work to do the conversion, especially when "high-performance" is a part of the project. Also, *refining* the conversion in order to make the car feel stock can take even more time than the basic engine conversion.

The V8 added about 100 lbs to the front end (compared to the Diesel), and the six-speed transmission added another 75 lbs (compared to the Volvo manual transmission). To improve weight distribution, the battery was relocated to the trunk, and a heavy-duty trailer hitch was installed. The 3500 lb Volvo averages 18–20 mpg, compared to 24–28 with the diesel. On freeway trips, the car now gets over 25 mpg. The engine turns 1500 rpm at 60 mph in sixth gear with the 3.54 axle ratio and 25" diameter tires. Performance (91 mph in the quarter mile) is very similar to an IROC Camaro with a 350 TPI , because a fully-optioned Camaro weighs about 3500 lbs. When the nitrous oxide system is activated, the Volvo is even quicker, but traction is a problem.

The performance of this conversion could easily be improved with the installation of a dual-catalytic converter exhaust system, aftermarket aluminum heads, high-performance cam, even a supercharger, all of which can be done legally with the smog-legal parts now on the market. Weight could also be easily and substantially reduced with a gear reduction starter, aluminum heads, the Borg-Warner six-speed used in the new Camaros and an Edelbrock long-style aluminum water pump (the only long-style aluminum water pump currently available).

If it sounds like we have big plans for this car, you should know that JTR plans to have a *Volvo 700 Series V8 Conversion Manual* available in December, 1994.

1981 CHEVROLET MALIBU STATION WAGON WITH 1990 305 TPI/700-R4

Due to the large number of people doing TPI engine swaps on the 1978-1987 G-body (El Camino, Malibu, Monte Carlo, Buick Regal, GMC Caballero, Oldsmobile Cutlass, Pontiac Grand Prix and Lemans), a chapter outlining the details of this swap are in this manual.

The engine shown above is actually from a Firebird. The Firebird TPI engine works better for this swap than the Camaro TPI engine because the air cleaner ducting and battery cables fit this chassis with no modifications. This is mostly a bolt-in conversion, but like any engine swap, there are a lot of details involved, and it can get quite costly.

Originally, this car had a 231 Buick V6, Turbo 350 transmission, and 2.73 gears. It averaged 18 mpg and would do 0-60 mph in 17 seconds. It was a dog. The V8 added about 140 lbs, but the wagon does 0-60 mph in about 9 seconds, and averages about 20 mpg. The 700-R4 overdrive transmission is greatly responsible for the improved gas mileage.

This is one of our own vehicles. It took over two weeks to complete the conversion, and cost about $1500 beyond the price of the engine/transmission. New exhaust, new radiator, new motor-mounts, shortened driveshaft, air-conditioning recharging, electric fuel pumps, and electric cooling fans were the major high cost items.

A lot of Street Rodders like the "Hi-Tech" look of the TPI engines, but just as importantly, they are tired of tinkering with carburetors.

The owner of this 1941 Chevrolet Business Coupe installed a 305 TPI/5-speed from a 1988 Camaro. He intends to use this vehicle as a daily driver (after it's painted!). Like most engine swaps, the owner has spent many hours and dollars just getting to this point. As with most car projects, the owner's wife hasn't been told just how much this has cost.

Because older cars such as this are exempt from California-style smog inspection programs, the owner decided to remove the smog pump for a cleaner looking engine compartment. "Block hugger" headers were installed because the Camaro exhaust manifolds would not clear the frame. The headers interfered with the knock sensor, so it was relocated onto the clutch release boss, which is located just above the oil filter. Because a hydraulic clutch is used in this vehicle, this did not cause a problem. The clutch pedal and clutch master cylinder are from a 1988 Jeep Cherokee, which work fine with the Camaro slave cylinder.

The block hugger headers also required some of the engine wiring to be relocated.

The owner will be installing air conditioning, so he specified an engine-driven cooling fan, which required an unusual, but effective solution for the air cleaner ducting, and MAF sensor mounting, which is shown in the chapter on air cleaners and ducting.

1983 JAGUAR XJ-S WITH 1990 CORVETTE ENGINE

This was one of the most difficult and expensive engine swap we had ever done, and at the same time, it was one of the best conversions. It looks stock, and it drives like it's stock, until you step hard on the gas. Due to the intricacies of this engine swap, many details of this vehicle will be shown in this manual as examples of solutions to the problems that arise during an engine swap.

The Corvette engine is considerably more difficult and costly to install into a Jaguar (and most cars and trucks) than a Camaro/Firebird TPI engine. We thought the conversion would take three weeks to complete, but it took over three months.

A lot of the extra time consisted of fabricating small brackets and waiting for special order items. 1990 and newer TPI engines use a different vehicle speed sensor than 1989 and older TPI engines. We "wasted" about 4 weeks and over $700 trying to "mechanically" couple the Jaguar and Corvette electric speedometer sending units.

We finally hired an electronics engineer. He solved the problem for us in about three hours with about $100 of electronics parts and $300 for consulting fees, far less expensive than our own fiasco. Stealth Conversions now sells the appropriate parts for this vehicle speed sensor.

We can now install a 1990 Corvette engine/transmission into a Jaguar in about 4 weeks (160 hours).

The moral of the story is: Corvette TPI engines require more work to install than Camaro TPI engines, and the first time you try to do something different, it will take much longer than first expected.

The general approach to this engine swap was to use as much as possible from the Corvette, and as many over the counter parts as possible to insure reliability and serviceability. We also wanted to maximize the power of the Corvette engine by utilizing cold air induction. To get the cold air to the air cleaner, a narrower than normal radiator (at least for Jaguar V8 conversions) was required. It turned out that the radiator from the 1990 Corvette was two inches narrower than the usual Camaro radiator that is normally used for the Jaguar V8 engine swap. The radiator was offset to the driver's side to allow the 1988 Firebird TPI air cleaner snout to poke forward to get cold air. The air conditioning condenser was relocated about 1-1/2" to the driver's side for the cold air induction, and about 3/4" rearward to make room for the front-mounted electric cooling fan.

A 1990 Corvette "high-fill" cooling system surge tank was installed, requiring the relocation of the Jaguar windshield washer reservoir.

The high-pressure side of the air conditioning hoses has pressure switches to operate the electric fans and high-pressure safety shut-off switch.

The air cleaner ducting, hose routing, and wiring routing allow for normal engine movement, which is an important consideration in any engine swap. Engines are rubber mounted and do move around quite a bit during normal operation. All hoses, wiring, and air-cleaner ducting connected to the engine must be installed to allow for engine movement or they will fail.

I NEED MORE ROOM, GET ME A BIGGER HAMMER

We put a 350 TPI engine/700-R4 transmission from a 1989 Camaro into this 1985 S-10 4X4 Blazer for a magazine article. As you can see, it's a very tight fit, but the pry bar our chief mechanic is using is not really needed. Due to space limitations, cooling is the biggest problem with V8-powered S-10 trucks. There is not much room for a radiator and an engine-driven fan. A lot of the information in the chapter on cooling came from these types of conversions.

The wiring on this conversion was not difficult, it was the air cleaner ducting and cooling system that was tedious and time consuming. The conversion took three weeks to complete, and we knew what we were doing.

With the original carbureted 2.8 V6, 700-R4 transmission and 4.11 gears, this truck averaged about 18 mpg, and took forever to do 0-60 mph. The truck now averages about 15 mpg under similar driving conditions, but it is a lot more powerful and drivability is much better than the original engine. Installing 3.42 gears would probably bring the average gas mileage up to 18 mpg.

It is interesting to note that we have seen very little difference in gas mileage between 305 and 350 engines in comparable swaps, but there is a noticeable difference in performance.

At the time of this writing, this vehicle has been driven over 30,000 miles. It's been used for towing, trips, commuting, and ranch work, which includes rounding up cattle (cow-punching is not included in normal gas mileage figures). The 350 TPI has not compromised the usefulness of this vehicle at all. In fact, it's made this vehicle more useful.

To prove the strength of the drivetrain for our *Chevrolet S-10 Truck V8 Conversion Manual*, we installed an NOS brand nitrous oxide injection system, and ran it in the quarter mile. In 4-wheel-drive high range, it ran 13.7 seconds at 95 m.p.h. with Goodyear 235/75-R15 All Terrain tires. Remember, this is a 4X4 with skid plates, heavy off-road tires, a 2-speed transfer case, and stock suspension. What amazed most people is that the stock axles and transfer case have handled the power without breakage.

In case you're wondering about the custom wheels, they are off of a 1990 Jaguar XJ-6, and they bolted on with no adapters or spacers.

This conversion worked so well that similar vehicles are being used by undercover law enforcement officers in our area. Cops like quick vehicles, and have vast resources, otherwise known as confiscated property.

FULL SIZE TRUCK

This 1982 Chevrolet K5 Blazer has a TPI engine from a Firebird. This kind of swap is relatively easy because of the amount of room in the engine compartment, and the fact that the Camaro/Firebird accessories bolt up to the truck. The air conditioning condenser was flipped around so that the hose connections were on the passenger's side. The air conditioning hoses and power steering hoses from the Camaro/Firebird required some bending to fit the truck. The battery was moved to the driver's side to make room for the air cleaner and ducting. The exhaust manifolds from the TPI engine have the same basic shape as the truck's original exhaust manifolds, but the outlets have three bolts compared to two bolts used on the Camaro/Firebird engine. The flanges on the headpipes were changed and the exhaust from the truck fit right up to the TBI engine. The electric cooling fans from the Firebird were adapted to the truck and do an adequate job of cooling for non-towing applications. For towing applications, however, an engine-driven cooling fan is required.

1959 JEEP WITH TPI ENGINE

The buildup of this vehicle took the owner several years. There are many subtle custom modifications that are not related to the engine. For example, the headlights were "bug eyed" (moved forward), to allow moving the radiator forward so that the engine could be moved forward to improve driveline angles. The rectangular steel frame is completely airtight, and acts as an air storage tank for the engine-driven air compressor (for operating air-driven tools when off-roading). The rear wheel tubs were chamfered to allow the custom seats to recline. Power steering was added (visible behind the front bumper). A dual master cylinder was installed to improve the reliability of the brake system.

The purpose of the above is to point out that many engine swaps become much more than just an engine swap as the vehicle is customized. If you want to finish the engine swap in a timely manner, refrain from the "custom" mods that are not related to the engine swap until *after* the engine swap is complete.

The TPI portion of the vehicle required substantial amounts of time and money. The owner did not purchase a complete engine to do the installation. Instead, he purchased the TPI intake, wiring, computer, and other components, and installed them onto his older engine. He ran into some problems, but eventually got it running properly. He freely admits the swap would have been cheaper and easier if he had bought a *complete* engine for the installation.

1983 Chevrolet El Camino with 1989 350 TPI/700-R4.

This vehicle originally had a 231 Buick V6/Turbo 350 transmission.

This owner purchased the TPI engine/700-R4 transmission with the idea that the conversion would take about 4 days, and would cost little more than the cost of the engine and transmission.

It was over two months before the owner drove the car again, and it cost about $1500 (over the cost of the engine and transmission) to complete.

The "hidden" costs include: complete exhaust system, towing to the muffler shop, driveshaft shortening and balancing, fuel tank, air-conditioning evacuation and charge, radiator modifications, electric cooling fans, new front springs, etc.

The owner is pleased with his conversion and thinks he could now do the conversion in about a month (in his spare time), but it would still cost the same.

This vehicle gets the same overall gas mileage as the original 231 V6. The main reason for the similar fuel mileage with the bigger engine is the 700-R4 overdrive transmission.

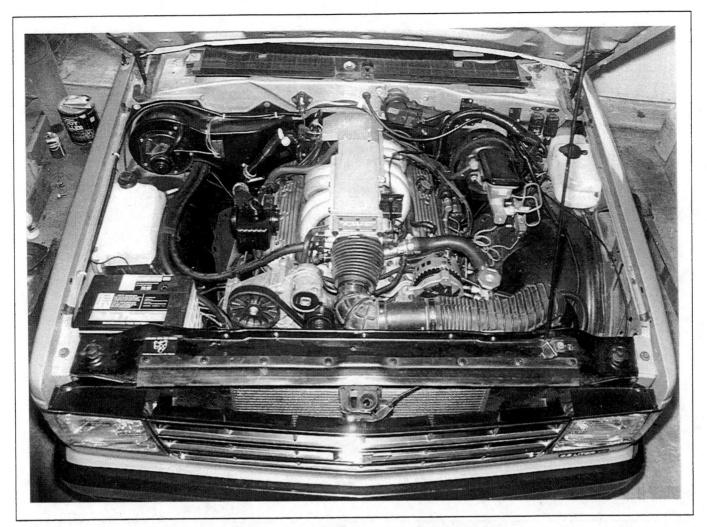

1985 Chevrolet S-10 TRUCK WITH 1989 305 TPI/700-R4 TRANSMISSION

This truck is lightweight (about 3,000 lbs.) and quick. The conversion is so sanitary that many people think this is a factory installed V8. The lack of air conditioning makes this conversion look easy.

The owner of this vehicle carefully prepared several weeks in advance to do the engine swap. He got everything needed for the conversion before he removed the stock motor, and he took a week off of work to do the conversion.

The owner had never before worked on fuel-injected engines, but he is knowledgeable in mechanics and electrical. He also studied the factory shop manuals and our *Chevrolet S-10 Truck V8 Conversion Manual*. It took less than a week from the time he removed the stock motor until the time the truck was running with V8 power. Still, it took several weeks to *completely* finish all the details on this conversion.

This is rare and exceptional among engine swaps. The key reasons for this kind of success are preparation, dedication, and experience. And of course, JTR's *Chevrolet S-10 Truck V8 Conversion Manual*.

FRIENDS DON'T LET FRIENDS DRIVE FORDS!

This 1984 Mustang SVO is now powered by a 1990 350 TPI/700-R4.

We don't believe there will be a lot of Mustang owners wanting to do this conversion, but this does illustrate that most engine swaps have a lot of similarities and requirements. What was really amazing to us is the dimensional similarity between Mustangs and Camaros. For example, the Camaro radiator fit into the Mudstain quite easily. The engine/transmission dropped in with no sheet metal modifications. There are some areas that are really tight, but this is typical of most engine swaps. The cost to do the conversion was typical of most conversions...a lot more than the owner originally expected.

1991 Jeep Wrangler with 1990 Chevrolet 350 TBI

This vehicle is owned by an off-road accessory company, and will be used to display their products. The engine is from a 1990 full-size truck. The engine was installed complete with all of the Chevrolet truck accessories and exhaust manifolds.

The Jeep originally had an injected 2.5 liter 4-cylinder engine. Surprisingly, the 4-cylinder in-tank electric fuel pump has adequate capacity and pressure for the 350 V8.

Chevrolet-powered Jeeps are quite popular. The fuel-injection greatly improves the off-roading ability because the engine does not suffer from fuel starvation during off-road maneuvers the way carbureted engines often do.

For off-roading, the throttle-body-injected engines are often preferred over the TPI engines because of their lower idle speeds and better low speed torque, which makes for better rock crawling abilities.

DOUBLE WARNING

We made a bet with one of our consultants that we could complete a Volvo 240 V8 conversion in less than 6 weeks. We lost the bet, and the car has been sitting in our shop for over 5 months.

If only we would listen to our own advice!

We had seen and driven other Volvo 240 models with Chevrolet V8 engines. The conversion looked pretty darn easy. The first warning is: Typical of most engine swaps, it has taken a lot more time than originally planned, the cost has climbed higher than originally estimated[1], and other projects became more important.

This 1983 Volvo originaly came with a diesel, and is now *fitted* with a 1991 Camaro 305 TBI/700-R4 transmission. The engine swap looks simple and uncluttered because it is not completed; it is only being *fitted* in this photograph. When the spark plug wires, heater hoses, air-conditioning hoses, windshield washer bottle, coolant recovery tank, and wiring are finished, the engine compartment will look less simple.

The second warning is: You shouldn't race Volvos with diesel emblems, especially if they don't smoke. This particular Volvo is fitted with a NOS® throttle-body nitrous oxide injection system for drivetrain durability testing.

JTR's *Volvo 200 Series V8 Conversion Manual* should be available in June, 1994.

1.Because of the bet.

JIGGERS—IT'S A COP!!!

The person trying to hide his face is our consultant for the TPI/TBI installations. Normally he works for a law enforcement agency.

His older, government issued Caprice has a "quasi-government issued" Tuned Port Injection motor lurking under the hood. "Quasi-government issued" has something to do with vehicles that are confiscated in drug raids. This was the first TPI engine swap we had seen.

After this photo was taken, our consultant's Caprice was totalled when it was involved in a law enforcement "incident". Luckily, our consultant wasn't hurt.

In case you are wondering what our consultant is driving now, it is a Volvo similar to the TPI Volvo shown earlier in this book. He said something about it being "a good car to crash."

INTRODUCTION
Note Page

ENGINES

People often ask us what engine we recommend for engine swaps. The simple answer is: The newer, the better. When we do engine swaps, we don't want to rebuild the engine. It is a lot cheaper to buy a relatively new, but more expensive engine than it is to buy an old, worn out engine and rebuild it.

The late model fuel-injected engines will easily run in excess of 200,000 miles when properly maintained. They are that good. One of the reasons they last so long is because the fuel/air ratio is so precisely controlled that the oil is not washed off the cylinder walls from running too rich, and reduced blowby from less cylinder wear keeps the oil cleaner. Another reason is the reduced engine speed from the overdrive transmissions. Still another reason is that the engine oils have improved.

If you are considering a TBI truck engine for your light-duty vehicle, avoid the 8600 GVW (Gross Vehicle Weight Rating) 3/4 ton, and one ton truck engines because they have less power and fuel economy than the 7200 GVW 3/4 ton truck engines, and the 1/2 ton truck engines. This is because the heavy-duty truck engines (GVW of 8600 lbs. and over) are designed for sustained full-throttle usage, and are equipped with lower compression, larger valve stems, and smaller valves. They are great for heavy-duty usage, but in light-duty applications, you will be happier with the light-duty engines.

For engine swaps where you want low cost and reliability, and the "Hi-Tech" look is not important, we prefer the TBI engines over the TPI engines. We strongly feel that the TBI engines are highly under-rated because they lack the "Look" of the TPI engines. We typically install TPI engines into our own vehicles for magazine and marketing reasons. In many of our TPI-powered vehicles, we would have been happier with TBI engines because of the money we would have saved.

Compared to a TPI engine, a typical TBI engine uses a milder cam, and idles at about 550 rpm, compared to 700 rpm for a typical TPI engine. The typical TBI engine has plenty of power just above idle, the typical TPI engine doesn't come on strong until about 2200 rpm. The typical 700 rpm idle of the TPI engine causes automatic transmissions vehicles to "creep" slightly at idle. The TBI engines get marginally better fuel mileage than the TPI engines, mostly because of the milder cam timing, and TBI engines cost a lot less than TPI engines at the wrecking yards.

There are a lot of similarities between the Throttle Body Injection and the Tuned Port Injection. Both systems use many of the same sensors, wiring, and components. The biggest difference between the two systems is that the TBI has two large injectors mounted on top of the intake manifold. The TPI system uses 8 injectors—one mounted near each intake valve.

Theoretically, the TPI offers better fuel distribution because each cylinder gets its own injector. In reality, the TBI system offers good fuel distribution, and in our opinion, the theoretical fuel distribution differences between TPI and TBI are mostly academic.

When comparing the difficulty of installing a Camaro TBI versus a Camaro TPI engine, the TPI engine is more difficult to install because of the remote air cleaner and ducting. The air cleaner ducting is normally in the way of an engine-driven fan, so electric cooling fans are normally installed. Electric cooling fans do not move as much air as engine driven fans, hence, the cooling system usually requires more attention (money) than when installing a TBI engine. Other than the air cleaner ducting and its relationship with the cooling system, there is very little difference between installing a TPI engine or a TBI engine.

ENGINES

BEWARE OF THE CORVETTE ENGINES

Generally speaking, it is easier to install the Camaro/Firebird TPI engines into most cars and trucks than it is to install the Corvette TPI engines. Corvette engines are different than Camaro/Firebird engines in a number of ways that can increase the difficulty of an engine swap.

As an example, the 1990 Corvette engine in the 1983 Jaguar XJ-S shown in the introduction required the following additional work, as compared to installing a 1990 Camaro TPI engine:

1. The wiring harness is considerably more difficult to work with than the Camaro/Firebird wiring harness. To the novice, the wires seem to go everywhere. Even to the experienced, the wires seem to go everywhere.

2. The 1990-1991 Corvette ECM (Engine Control Module, or computer) is mounted in the engine compartment. The Jaguar (and many other cars) does not have room in the engine compartment to mount the ECM, so all of the wires to the ECM had to be lengthened to mount the ECM outside of the engine compartment. On 1985-1989 Corvettes, the "trunk" of the wiring harness is not as long as the "trunk" on Camaro/Firebird wiring harnesses, so the wiring harness may need to be extended to mount the ECM in many engine swaps.

3. The power steering pump uses a remote reservoir which needed custom brackets to mount to the Jaguar. The power steering pump could not use a standard hose that is normally used on Jaguars, or other cars.

4. The oil pan and pick-up tube had to be replaced with a Camaro oil pan and pick-up tube to clear the Jaguar crossmember.

5. The driver's side exhaust manifold interfered with the steering shaft. Replacing the exhaust manifold required modifications to the alternator bracket.

6. The 1990-1992 Corvette cooling system uses a "high-fill" surge tank in addition to a coolant recovery tank. These required mounting, and required additional hoses. This took more space.

7. The Corvette air conditioning compressor does not have a high pressure cut-out switch, so one had to be installed into the air conditioning hose. Camaro/Firebird engines have the high-pressure cut-out switch mounted on the compressor.

8. The Chevy-Jag motor mount required slight modifications to accommodate the bracket for the power steering pump.

9. The wiring for the electric cooling fans and relays is not incorporated into the Corvette engine wiring harness. Camaro/Firebird engines have the electric wiring for the electric cooling fans and relays incorporated into the engine wiring harness.

10. The wiring for the alternator and charcoal canister are not incorporated into the engine wiring harness. Camaro/Firebird TPI engines have the alternator and charcoal canister wiring incorporated into the engine wiring harness.

11. 1986-1989 Corvettes require a switch on the shift linkage (automatic transmission) to let the ECM know when the shift lever is in the overdrive position, Camaro/Firebird TPI engines do not use such a switch.

12. 1985-1988 TPI engines use a cold start injector. Corvettes do not have the wiring for the cold start injector incorporated into the engine wiring harness. Camaro/Firebird engines have the electric wiring for the cold start injector incorporated into the engine wiring harness.

It may not seem like a lot from the above description, but believe us, the Corvette engine is a lot more difficult to install in most engine swaps than a Camaro/Firebird engine. The people who *try* to install the Corvette engines into other cars are so overwhelmed by all of the details required, that a lot of mistakes are made, and it normally takes the owner quite a while to sort all of the bugs out of the engine swap.

ENGINES
Note Page

CAMARO/FIREBIRD TPI ENGINE

For most TPI engine swaps, this is the engine of choice. It will fit into most vehicles that already have a Chevrolet small block V8 with a minimum of modifications and additional expenses. 1990–1992 engines don't have MAF sensors, which simplifies air cleaner mounting and ducting.

Often, the power steering hoses, exhaust manifolds, motor mounts, and oil pan can be used in another chassis.

The above engine is a 1988 350 fitted with the optional oil cooler. The lines carry engine coolant, not oil.

The oil temperature is controlled by the engine coolant, and in the winter, the "oil cooler" actually brings the oil *up* to operating temperature.

The motor mount shown is for a 2WD S-10 V8 conversion.

1990 CORVETTE ENGINE, DRIVER'S SIDE

Compared to the Camaro engine shown on the previous page, the Corvette engine differs in the following areas:

1. Oil pan and pick-up tube (see page 2–15).

2. Belt driven accessories and brackets (see pages 2–13).

3. Exhaust manifolds are made of tubular steel and are of a completely different design than those used on Camaros.

4. Engine wiring harness is completely different than the Camaro harness in terms of routing and general layout. 1990-1992 Corvettes have the ECM mounted in the engine compartment, and the connectors to the ECM have weather-tight seals. The "trunk" of the harness is much shorter than a Camaro harness, and must be lengthened for the ECM to be placed in the passenger compartment.

5. "Big" HEI distributor and 8mm. spark plug wires are used on all TPI Corvettes. "Small" HEI distributor is used on 1987 and newer Camaros.

6. Oil temperature sending unit is used on Corvette engines, Camaro has never used an oil temperature sensor.

7. Oil pressure switches and sending units are mounted near the distributor. 1989-1992 Camaro engines have the oil pressure switch/sending unit mounted just above the oil filter.

8. Plumbing for the oil cooler is different than the (optional) oil cooler used on the Camaros.

CAMARO ENGINE, PASSENGER'S SIDE

WEIGHT

A fully dressed 1990 Corvette engine/700-R4 transmission, complete with wiring harness, ECM, engine and transmission oil, weighs about 725 lbs.

A similarly dressed 1990 Camaro 305 TPI engine/Automatic transmission weighs about 795 lbs.

Weight savings (all numbers are approximate):

1. Aluminum heads   40 lbs.
2. Gear reduction starter   9 lbs.
3. Aluminum water pump   6 lbs.
4. Exhaust manifolds   10 lbs.
5. Air conditioning compressor   5 lbs.

1990 CORVETTE ENGINE, PASSENGER'S SIDE, 1985-1991 SIMILAR

Compared to a Camaro engine, the Corvette engine differs in the following ways:

1. Gear reduction starter is used on 1988-1991 models.

2. Aluminum heads with angled spark plugs are used on 1986-1/2 through 1991 models.

3. Air conditioning compressor is a Nippondenso unit (1988-1991).

4. External EGR tube. Aluminum heads have no exhaust cross-over passages (see page 2–16).

5. Fuel lines exit on passenger's side of engine. Camaro's exit on driver's side of engine.

6. Intake manifold has a coolant fitting designed to de-aerate the coolant (see page 2–16).

7. The plenum extension cover over the distributor (not installed in this photo) is made of aluminum. Camaros use a plastic cover.

8. The oil filler cap is on the passenger's side valve cover.

CAMARO/FIREBIRD TPI ENGINE, 1985–1987

Notice all of the fan belts. Some people like all of the fan belts because they feel that if one belt breaks, the water pump will still turn and the engine can still run. They also feel that if an accessory fails (as in seizes), the fan belt can be removed from the offending accessory, and the vehicle can still be driven.

The above engine is a 1987, the only difference between the above engine accessories compared to the 1985-1986 Camaro/Firebird engines is that the 1985-1986 engines use the older, and physically larger 10-SI alternator, and a different upper alternator bracket.

CAMARO/FIREBIRD ENGINE, 1988–1992, FRONT VIEW

Notice the serpentine belt and the simpler brackets for mounting the accessories, when compared to the 1985-1987 engines.

With this set-up, the water pump can be replaced without removing any other accessories.

For some reason, 1988 engines use a different fan belt routing than 1989-1992 engines, even though the accessories are in the same location. Also, some of the reinforcement brackets for the accessories were added and deleted throughout the 1988-1992 model years.

FAN BELTS

1985-1987 Camaro/Firebird V8s use multiple fan belts which can affect fan clearance on vehicles with short engine compartments such as the Chevrolet S-10 Trucks. Often a fan spacer is required to keep the fan from contacting the fan belts and the accessories.

Installing a 1976-1981 Camaro/Caprice/Malibu alternator and air pump and their associated pulleys and brackets will improve fan clearance by over an inch. The switching valve for the air pump can be bolted onto the older pump position with some minor hose rerouting and bracket bending.

On the S-10 Trucks, the older accessories can mean the difference between driveshaft modifications required when the engine is moved rearward for fan/radiator clearance and no driveshaft modifications with adequate fan clearance.

SERPENTINE BELTS AND CUSTOM LENGTHS

On this 1988 Camaro TPI engine, the power steering pump and the AIR (smog) pump have been removed.

A shorter serpentine belt was obtained (Goodyear 4060805) at an auto parts store to drive the remaining accessories.

Serpentine belts are generally available in 3/4" increments from most auto parts stores, so there should be no problem getting the correct belts for most custom applications.

The belt tensioner has markings on it that show if the belt is too long or too short. Refer to the shop manual (from Helm) in section 6B (cooling and radiator) for more information.

If you want to remove the air conditioning compressor, install the idler pulley used on non-air conditioned Camaro/Firebirds.

If you want to remove the AIR smog pump and keep the power steering pump, use Goodyear part # 4060967.

CORVETTE ACCESSORIES, 1985-1987

Notice the position of the air conditioning compressor, as compared to the 1988-1991 Corvette engine. Notice how the accessories are positioned for the lower hood line used in the Corvette, as compared to the Camaro engine accessories.

The dark cylindrical container on the far right side of the engine is the remote power steering reservoir.

CORVETTE ENGINE, 1988–1991

Notice how low the accessories are mounted, and the width of this set-up. This set-up will not fit in a narrow engine compartment. The large pulley-like object covering/hiding the aluminum water pump is a weight ring designed to reduce harmonics (vibration) in the serpentine belt at high engine speeds. It is called a dampener. It is needed on this accessory drive because of the long, unsupported belt distance to the air conditioning compressor.

Note: Fan belt vibrations can literally destroy accessory brackets and accessories. We know several people who continually have alternator problems or brackets breaking. The cause of the problem is that the belt vibration literally shakes the alternator apart or fatigues the brackets. Solutions to these problems include adding idler pulleys to support the fan belt, adding extra braces to support the accessories, or adding a dampener.

CORVETTES ENGINES

Because of the oil temperature sending unit located near the oil filter, Corvette engines use a "tee" to mount the oil pressure sending unit and the oil pressure switch (for the fuel pump) on the back of the engine.

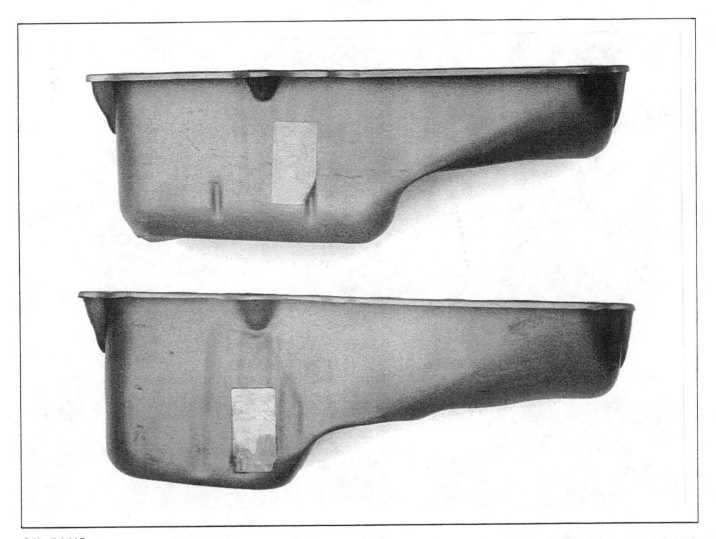

OIL PANS

The upper oil pan is used in 1986-1991 Corvettes. The 1984-1985 Corvette pan is the same except for the rear oil seal design.

The lower oil pan is used in 1986-1982 Camaros. The 1982-1985 Camaro pan is the same except for the rear oil seal design.

The Corvette oil pan offers 3/4" better ground clearance than the Camaro pan, but the sump extends about 3" more forward, which can interfere with crossmembers or steering linkages in many applications. The Corvette oil pan and pick-up tube is ideal for a V8 Datsun Z (did you know that JTR sells a V8 Conversion manual for 1970-1978 Datsun Z cars?).

The Corvette pan places the oil pick-up tube more forward than the Camaro pan, and a windage tray is installed in the Corvette engine, but none is used in the Camaro engine.

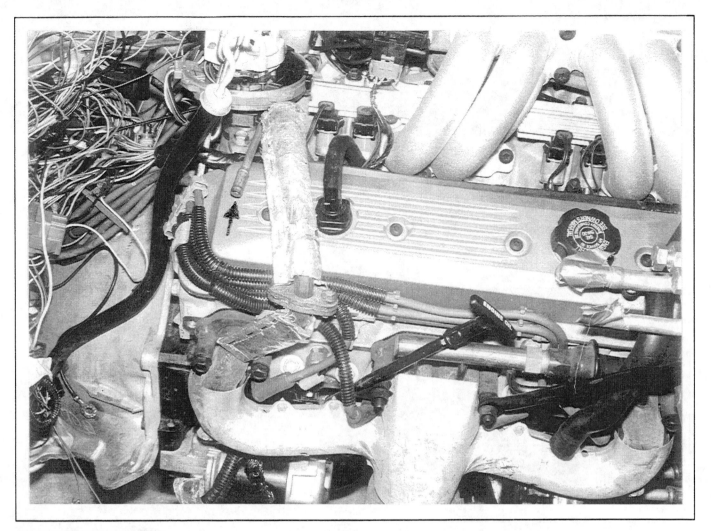

CORVETTE ENGINES

Other unique features of the Corvette engines are:

1. External EGR (1986-1991). The insulated tube going from the rear of the exhaust manifold, over the valve cover and into the intake manifold is for the EGR (Exhaust Gas Recirculation). The Corvette aluminum cylinder heads have no exhaust crossover passages, so the only way to run the exhaust gases into the intake manifold is through the external EGR tube.

   The difficulties of the External EGR come into play for those wanting to use headers on their engine swap because an external EGR tube will have to be installed onto the header. Many engine swappers want the engine compartment to look as simple as possible and don't want to run the external EGR tube. Without changing the PROM in the ECM or grounding the park-neutral wire, the "Check Engine" light will be turned on.

2. The small metal tube (arrow), next to the external EGR tube is for the Corvette cooling system. It connects to the "high fill reservoir" and allows steam to escape from the back of the block and improves cooling under extreme conditions. It also allows quick filling the cooling system because all the air can quickly escape from the cooling system passages.

ENGINES
Note Page

This is the rear view of a 1988 Camaro TPI engine (TBI engine is similar).

The oil pressure fuel pump switch (arrow), sticks out of the left side of the engine quite a bit, and may cause interference in some installations. If this is a problem for your engine swap, install the oil pressure switch, and the oil pressure sending unit used on 1985-1991 Corvettes (shown on page 2–14).

If the switches and sending units are changed, the wires will have to be rerouted.

If the fuel pump relay fails, the oil pressure switch will turn on the fuel pump after a few seconds of engine cranking. If your fuel-injected engine takes more than a couple of seconds of cranking to start, it's a good bet the fuel pump relay needs to be replaced. Most people believe the oil pressure switch is to shut off the fuel pump in case the engine loses oil pressure, but this is not the case on the TPI and TBI engines.

1988 CAMARO ENGINE WITH WIRING HARNESS REROUTED

The wiring harness along the rear of the engine is quite bulky, and may cause interference problems on some engine swaps. Here the wiring harness has been rerouted upward and forward to improve firewall/transmission tunnel clearance. This is a fairly common requirement for many TPI/TBI engine swaps which offer limited firewall or transmission tunnel clearance. This modification is required on 1978-1987 G-Bodies (Malibu, El Camino, Monte Carlo, etc.) and S-10 Trucks.

The wires to the transmission TCC (Torque Converter Clutch), VSS (Vehicle Speed Sensor), and the wires to the oil pressure sending unit/fuel pump switch, oxygen sensor, and water temperature sending unit must each be extended about 6 inches.

Camaro engines have the tubing for the air injection routed behind the engine, and on vehicles with limited firewall clearance, we normally replace it with 5/8" i.d. rubber air injection hose and route it for better firewall clearance. The tubing for the air injection has been removed in the above photograph.

On Corvette engines, the air injection plumbing is routed along the front of the engine.

To further improve firewall clearance on some engine swaps, (such as the S-10 truck V8 conversion,) reposition the distributor by 45° clockwise, and move the spark wires over by one position. This will move the connectors on the back of the distributor away from the firewall.

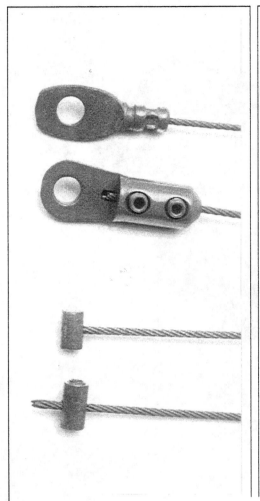

THROTTLE CABLES

1985–1989 TPI engines use the throttle cable ends shown on top. The very top fitting is stock. The second fitting is from a Lokar "Hi Tech" TPI throttle cable kit. It installs easily and securely onto almost any throttle cable with two set screws when you can't use the stock throttle cable.

1990–1992 TPI engines use the throttle cable ends shown on the bottom. The very bottom fitting is also from Lokar's "Hi Tech" TPI throttle cable kit.

Due to the geometry of the stock throttle linkage, getting full throttle travel puts a lot of stress on the cable. The geometry can be changed by relocating the cable upwards (as shown above) where it goes through the bracket for the TV (Throttle Valve) cable, cruise control cable, and throttle cable. This will allow full throttle travel with less stress on the cable.

On TBI engines, we recommend using an Edelbrock throttle cable bracket (part #8036) for most engine swaps. The Edelbrock throttle cable bracket also has provisions for the transmission throttle valve cable and the cruise control cable.

The Edelbrock and Lokar products are available from auto parts stores, and mail order stores.

INSTALLING TPI ONTO OLDER ENGINES

Generally, installing the Chevrolet fuel-injection onto an engine that was not originally fuel-injected can be more expensive than purchasing a **complete** fuel-injected engine at the wrecking yard. We often see the TPI intake manifolds and wiring harnesses at swap meets. The prices vary from quite reasonable to quite unreasonable. The biggest problem we see with the swap meet "bargains" is that a lot of the parts are missing or damaged. The seller often does not know what the system came off of.

The real problem is for the potential buyer. A person inexperienced with the fuel-injection system does not know about all of the parts required for the fuel-injection system, and cannot appreciate the advantages of buying a complete engine with all of the accessories and components that make up a complete fuel-injection system. Most importantly about the "swap meet systems" is that the seller probably bought the system on an impulse the year before, and it has been sitting around in his garage collecting dust and losing parts. And the seller probably purchased the system from somebody who bought the system on an impulse two years before, and it sat in his garage collecting dust and losing parts.

We have seen people purchase the "fuel-injection parts" for a TPI engine with the idea of installing them on their older engines, yet we have only seen a few of these projects make it to completion. Most of the "fuel-injection parts" type of projects are never completed. Of those people who had actually completed their projects, most of them said that they spent more on the cost of the "extras" than what they would have spent if they had bought a complete engine at the wrecking yard.

Installing the Chevrolet fuel-injection onto an engine that was not originally fuel-injected is often not as simple as it would first appear. Sometimes the accessories are not compatible with the fuel-injection. For example, many people with full size trucks that have TBI V8s want to install the TPI intake system. The problem with the TPI installation onto a TBI truck engine is that the accessory and fan belt routing will not allow for the air cleaner ducting, so the accessory brackets must be changed to the TPI Camaro configuration.

The air cleaner ducting and space requirements are the biggest problems involved with many of the TPI installations. If you plan on installing a TPI intake onto the engine in your vehicle, make sure that the accessories (alternator, air conditioning compressor, power steering pump, smog pump) and bracketry will not interfere with the TPI unit, or at least be prepared to make the necessary changes, and be prepared for the cost of these changes because they can be quite expensive. If you think that installing the brackets and accessories from a TPI Camaro or Corvette will solve the accessories problem, think again because *the newer engines have more bosses in the cylinder heads for mounting accessories than earlier engines.*

In addition to the possible problems with accessories, the fuel-injection system should be calibrated to the engine combination it will be installed on, just like a carburetor should be calibrated to the engine it will be installed on. The stock Chevrolet fuel-injection is somewhat adaptable to engine variations, and will work on different engine combinations, but it works best when it is used on the engine it was originally designed for.

INSTALLING TPI ONTO OLDER ENGINES

For those who are installing a fuel-injection system onto an engine that was not injected, a Chevrolet parts book (available from your friendly Chevrolet parts counter person) will help greatly at tracking down parts which will be required. And believe us when we say that you will be requiring parts that did not come with the unit you bought. (Chevrolet will be discontinuing paper parts books. Newer parts catalogs will be on microfische or on computer disks.)

BASIC MECHANICAL DIFFERENCES

The biggest problem with installing the 1987 and newer Camaro intake manifolds onto older engines is that four of the mounting bolt holes do not line up with the 1986 and older heads. You must grind or file the holes in the intake manifold so the bolts will line up properly. Large washers are then installed to cover up the elongated holes.

DISTRIBUTOR DRIVE GEARS

It is important to use the correct distributor drive gear so that it matches the camshaft. The distributors in engines with factory roller cams use different distributor drive gears than the older engines. The distributor drive gears look the same, but the roller cams are made of harder steel than the non-roller cams, which requires the different distributor drive gear for proper wear characteristics. The metallurgy of the distributor drive gears is different. There is a lot more to engine building than most people can imagine; metallurgy, lubrication, and wear are only a few of the factors involved in engineering different parts for engines. Any time something is changed, other problems can appear, which is why we recommend that you purchase a complete, matched engine for your TPI/TBI engine swap.

GETTING IT BIGGER

Let's say that you have a 305 TPI or TBI engine and you decide to replace the long-bock with a 350, 383, or 400 cubic inch long-block for more power.

While we have never done this, we recommend the following:

1. Replace the knock sensor and knock sensor module to that of a 350.

2. Replace the PROM to that of a 350, or use a custom aftermarket prom.

3. Replace the injectors to those from a 350, or increase the fuel pressure with an aftermarket fuel pressure regulator.

4. Modify the automatic transmission to shift properly with the larger engine.

PURCHASING AN ENGINE

Once again, we stress buying a **_COMPLETE_** engine. Complete means: intake manifold, oil pan, water pump, water pump pulley, starter motor, throttle body, wiring harness, exhaust manifolds, air pump, air conditioning compressor, power steering pump, distributor, valve covers, harmonic balancer, crank pulley, charcoal canister, computer, relays, wiring connectors, flex plate or fly-wheel... We hope you get the point.

Besides buying this book, buying the engine/transmission can be the single most important step for your engine swap (aren't we modest?). Buying a complete and matched engine and transmission will greatly simplify and ease your conversion by reducing parts chasing, and parts confusion caused by miss-matched parts. Avoid buying an engine that is missing "a few" parts. "A few" parts can end up costing quite "a few" dollars.

One more note about purchasing an engines: if your engine has some damaged or missing parts, do not mix & match sensors, relays, modules, or anything else.

We have a saying for those "pieced together" types of swaps:

"Mix & Match and you shall see,
It don't work as it's meant to be!"

DONOR CAR: 1990 CORVETTE WITH 6-SPEED TRANSMISSION

The engine and transmission in this car were not damaged, but the car is considered a total loss. The engine was quickly sold for about $3500, and the 6-speed transmission was *immediately* sold for $3,000*.

Finding a Corvette like this at the wrecking yard is rare, and the price of the parts is reflected by the rarity. A 1990 Camaro/Firebird with a 350/700-R4 is much more common, and would sell for considerably less.

Although there are a lot of Camaros in the background, many have V6 engines or carbureted V8s.

* Note: The 1993 Camaros have Borg-Warner 6-speed manual transmissions, which should reduce the value/novelty of the Corvette ZF 6-speed transmissions. The Camaro 6-speed will not have provisions for a speedometer cable. An electric speedometer will be required. At the time of this writing, Borg-Warner is looking at the possibility of selling the 6-speed transmission for aftermarket use. It will have provisions for a speedometer cable.

ACKNOWLEDGMENTS

To the previous owners of late model Camaros, Corvettes, and Firebirds who have so *skillfully* totalled their cars without damaging the engines and transmissions; Thanks for making the late model fuel-injected engines so readily available for engine swaps.

GET IT COMPLETE

The engine shown above is from a 1988 305/5-speed Firebird. When buying an engine, be sure to get the air cleaner, air cleaner ducting, and the charcoal canister with the solenoid valve. The Firebird air cleaner shown retails for over $200 (the 1985-1987 Firebird air-cleaner costs "only" $136!). The ducting is another $50 and the charcoal canister (including the solenoid valve) retails for about $95. Most people have no idea how expensive air cleaner parts can be, until they have to buy them.

It is a good idea to record the VIN numbers of the vehicle that the engine came from. The GM diagnostic system at the dealership can bring up all recalls and factory bulletins for the engine based on the VIN number. The GM system is very sophisticated and having the VIN number from the vehicle that the engine came from will make future services and repairs at the dealership much easier.

Another point: Notice how much room is required for the factory Firebird air cleaner and ducting. Before you buy an engine, read the chapter on air cleaners and ducting.

Reminder: These engines normally come out of vehicles that were totalled in some kind of impact, so don't assume that everything is OK!

PURCHASING AN ENGINE
Note Page

AUTOMATIC TRANSMISSIONS

To complement the low rpm drivability offered by the fuel-injected Chevrolet V8s we only recommend using the late model overdrive transmissions.

The 700-R4 automatic overdrive transmissions got a bad reputation because the early units (1982-1985) had some problems. The 1986 and newer 700-R4 transmissions are very reliable.

Using a Turbo-350 or Turbo-400 transmission will take away most of the highway fuel economy gains of the fuel-injection. The real beauty of the fuel-injected engines is how well they run at low engine speeds under load. Most of the new V8 cars and trucks are geared so that the engine runs between 1300 and 1700 rpm at 60 mph in overdrive. If you tried this with a non-computer controlled engine, the engine might stumble, or ping, or the low vacuum would cause the power valve circuit in the carburetor to open, destroying fuel economy. The fuel-injected engines thrive on low rpm cruising.

Most people believe that when a car is slowed down by downshifting, or using engine braking, it is the compression stroke that slows the vehicle, hence the term "compression braking". While this is partly true, the so called "compression braking" is really "engine friction braking."

A typical 350 V8 requires about 50 lb.-ft. of torque to rotate the crankshaft. In other words, the engine has 50 lb.-ft. of drag. At 5250 rpm, this equals 50 horsepower.

A typical car with 3.42 gears and 26" diameter tires with a Turbo-350 or Turbo-400 transmission would have the engine turning at 2650 rpm at 60 mph, assuming no torque converter slippage. Factor in about 250 rpm for torque converter slippage and the engine rpm at 60 mph is 2900. The friction drag of a 350 V8 is going to be about 27 horsepower. The same vehicle with a 700-R4 transmission and lock-up torque converter will be doing 1850 rpm at 60 mph. Engine-friction will be about 17 horsepower (assuming 50 lb.-ft. to rotate the engine).

The lock-up function of the torque converter is extremely beneficial on vehicles with low numerical rear axle ratios because an engine that would turn 1400 rpm at 60 mph in lock-up will typically turn 1750 rpm unlocked. Going uphill, or into a head wind will increase the slippage, and make an even greater difference.

If you are afraid that running the motor at such low speeds will cause engine damage, don't worry, we have *never* seen any engine damage caused by running an engine at low speeds.

To give an example of the fuel mileage difference the .70 overdrive ratio makes on freeway mileage, our Jaguar XJ-6 with 3.31 rear axle ratio gets about 17 mpg in third gear (direct drive) on freeway trips. In overdrive, the car gets 23 mpg with no other changes.

In final, why waste a good late model engine with an obsolete transmission. The overdrive transmissions are the only way to go!

AUTOMATIC TRANSMISSIONS

BUYING A 700-R4 TRANSMISSION

Do not use anything but the correctly matched 700-R4 transmission behind your TPI or TBI engine. Unless you are an expert at modifying a transmission's shift points for an engine's power curve, don't install anything except for the properly matched 700-R4 transmission behind your engine for best performance. Properly matched means the transmission is *exactly* the same transmission that the factory would have used with the engine you are using.

When we buy our engines, we always try to get it complete with the transmission still attached to the engine. That's one reason why our swaps work so well.

The one change we sometimes do for our own conversions is install a TPI torque converter onto a TBI engine/transmission package. The main reason we do this is for improved acceleration off the line, and to reduce "creeping" at idle. A Camaro TBI torque converter has a stall speed of around 1800 rpm. A TPI torque converter normally has a stall speed of about 2200 rpm. Because of the lock-up function of the torque converter, this modification does not seem to affect fuel economy.

We do not recommend this modification if the vehicle will be used for towing purposes because high stall speed torque converters generate more heat when the torque converter is not locked-up. During towing, the torque converter may be unlocked for long periods of time, resulting in excessive heat, and possibly a damaged transmission.

The torque converter lock-up is normally controlled by the ECM, but later model 700-R4 transmissions have a temperature switch that will automatically lock up the torque converter in overdrive if the transmission fluid gets too hot. To avoid an explanation that tends to confuse people and cause great debates, just understand this:

DO NOT TOW WHILE IN OVERDRIVE. TOW IN THIRD GEAR!

USING A TURBO-350 OR TURBO-400 TRANSMISSION BEHIND AN ENGINE DESIGNED FOR A 700-R4 TRANSMISSION

Many of you, for one reason or another will be using an obsolete Turbo-350 or Turbo-400 transmission, even though we just told you why the 700-R4 transmission works so well behind the fuel-injected engines.

The number one question that people ask us about using these *obsolete* transmissions is, "What do I do with the wires that would normally go to the transmission?"

The answer is: Look at the factory shop manual (from Helm) for the engine you will be using, and look at the wiring diagram for the lock-up torque converter. Since the *obsolete* transmissions don't have overdrive (or fourth gear), ground the wire if the fourth gear switch is open in fourth gear, and leave the fourth gear wire open (do not connect it to anything) if the fourth gear switch is closed in fourth gear.

As for the other wires going to the transmission, do not connect them to anything. If you have a Turbo-350 transmission with a lock-up torque converter, connect the wires for the lock-up torque converter using the information from the shop manual for the vehicle that the transmission came out of, and the shop manual for the vehicle that the engine came out of.

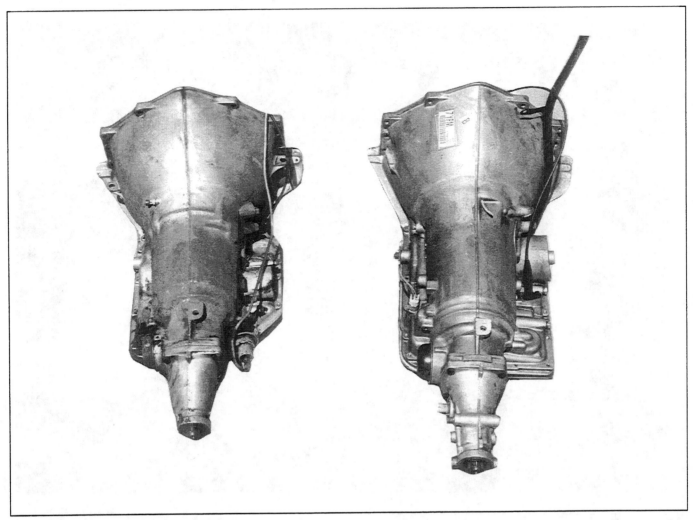

On the left is the Turbo-350 transmission which old-time hot rodders love and trust because it is inexpensive and common.

On the right is the 700-R4 transmission which is often misunderstood by old-time hot rodders because they have a lock-up torque converter and because the early units had some problems.

One common misconception about the 700-R4 is that the shifting is controlled by the engine computer (ECM). This is not true. The ECM does not control the gear changes. However, the ECM does control the lock-up torque converter. The 700-R4 transmission in non-computer controlled engines have the lock-up converter controlled by the valve body, or a vacuum switch combined with other electrical switches. (The 700–R4 transmissions used in the 1992 and newer trucks are completely controlled by the computer.)

The 700-R4 does not use a vacuum modulator. Instead, it uses a cable attached to the throttle linkage (called the TV cable or Throttle Valve cable) to control the shifting.

The 700-R4 is 3" longer than a short tailshaft Turbo-350 transmission and the right side of the 700-R4 sticks out a little further than the Turbo-350. The rear mounting pad is 1-3/4" further back than a Turbo-350. Both transmissions use the same style output shaft.

On the left is the 700-R4 transmission for a 60° V6. On the right is the 700-R4 transmission for a V8.

Many people who want to install V8s into S-10 trucks wrongly believe the 700-R4 behind the 2.8 V6 will bolt up to a V8.

Even if the V6 transmission would bolt up to the V8, we would not recommend it because the transmission is carefully calibrated for a specific engine and mismatching a transmission to an engine will result in poor shifts and possible transmission damage. Also, transmissions are not all wired the same inside, which will affect lock-up torque converter operation.

TAIL SHAFT HOUSINGS FOR THE 700-R4 TRANSMISSIONS

The upper tail shaft housing is for a 1982-1984 Caprice (GM part #8642231). A transmission mount will bolt to this tail housing and will allow bolting the 700-R4 transmission onto crossmembers designed for the 200-4R transmission used in the 1984-1988 G-bodies (El Camino, Monte Carlo, Buick Regal, Oldsmobile Cutlass, and Pontiac Grand Prix).

The transmission mount location will be the same as the rear mount position of a Turbo-400 transmission.

The lower tail housing is for a 1983-1992 Camaro. The 3 bosses are for mounting the torque arm and exhaust hanger.

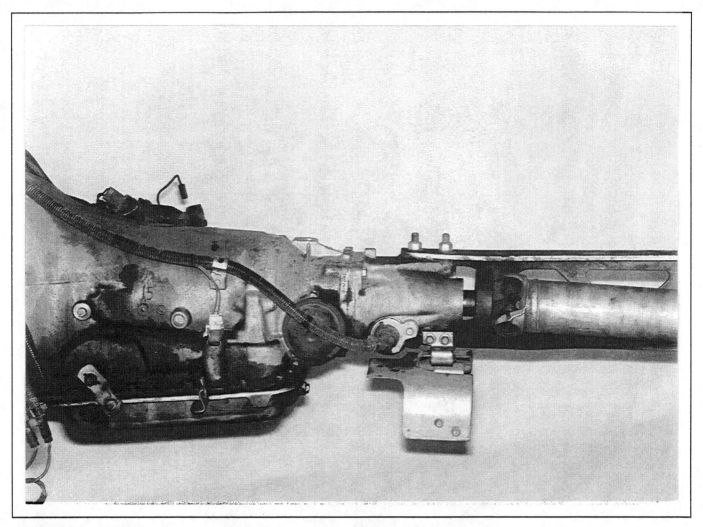

CORVETTE 700-R4

The Corvette uses a "backbone driveline beam" which connects the rear of the transmission to the differential. The Corvette transmission *case* does not have provisions for a conventional style of rear mount that is used on cars and trucks.

The tailhousing from a 1982-1984 Caprice (GM part #8642231) will allow installing a conventional transmission mount, but the location will be the same as the rear mount position of a Turbo-400 transmission, which may require crossmember modifications on some vehicles.

The Caprice tailhousing positions the speedometer gear differently than the Corvette tailhousing. Information about repositioning the speedometer gear on the Corvette output shaft is covered in the factory shop manual (available from Helm) in the chapter on automatic transmissions.

If you don't reposition the speedometer gear after changing the tailhousing, the speedometer gears will need replacing on a monthly basis! If you don't believe us, ask the owner of the Jaguar shown on page 1-6.

MANUAL TRANSMISSIONS

There are 4 different overdrive manual transmissions that are used behind the TPI and TBI small block V8s: The Borg-Warner T5 (used in the 1983-1992 Camaro/Firebird), the Doug Nash 4+3 (used in the 1984-1988 Corvette. It will be referred to as the "Corvette 4+3"), the ZF 6-speed (used in the 1989-1992 Corvette), the Muncie-Getrag (used in 1988-1992 1/2 ton full-size trucks and, with a slightly different case, in the 4.3 V6 S-Trucks).

The transmission on top is a Borg-Warner T5 transmission used in the 1983-1992 Camaro/Firebird models. The T5 transmission is used in other applications such as the Chevrolet S-10 trucks, Datsun 280 ZX Turbos, Ford Mustangs, and Jeeps, but they all use different mounting provisions, input shafts, output shafts, shifter positions, and will not interchange with the Camaro T5. The T5 used in the Mustang, Jeep, and Datsun ZX Turbo, all use the same bolt pattern to attach the transmission to the bell housing. The transmission on the bottom is from a 1984-1988 Corvette. It is a 4-speed manual transmission with an electrically shifted overdrive unit mounted on the rear.

The overdrive works in second, third and fourth gears, which is why it is called the 4+3 (four forward gears plus three more with overdrive).

The Camaro V8 5-speed is a great transmission if you are not running a lot of horsepower. It is easy to shift, light weight (87 lbs. as shown), quiet, and has good gear ratios. It is used behind the 305 TPI and TBI engines, but it is not used behind the 350 TPI engine, so use that as an indication of how much power (abuse) it will handle.

The 1988 and newer Camaro V8 5-speeds are called "World Class" T5 transmissions. The World Class transmissions feature improved bearings and organic (paper cone) synchronizers. Use only Dexron 2 automatic transmission fluid or other approved lubricants in the World Class transmissions or the organic synchronizers may get damaged by reacting with the oil.

The T5 is available with two different overdrive ratios, either .73:1 or .63:1. In general, the .63 overdrive ratio was used in all TBI engines and the TPI engines without engine oil coolers. The .73 overdrive ratio was used behind all TPI engines with oil coolers. The T5 transmission is rated for 300 ft-lb of torque.

MANUAL TRANSMISSIONS

CORVETTE 4+3 TRANSMISSION

The Corvette 4+3 transmission was used in 1984-1988 Corvettes. It is basically a Borg-Warner Super T-10 4-speed with an electrically shifted overdrive unit on the back. The overdrive unit is much like an automatic transmission; it uses automatic transmission fluid and routes it through an oil cooler. The overdrive ratio is usually .68:1, but some units came with a .60:1 ratio. The transmission is fairly heavy (133 lbs. as shown) and heavy shifting. When it first came out, we thought it was the greatest transmission available because it was the only available overdrive transmission that could handle a lot of horsepower. After some time, we learned that the 4+3 transmission is a complex unit and the overdrive units had their share of problems and were very expensive to repair. At that time, the Borg-Warner T5 was not doing real well. The World Class T5 transmission is much improved over the early units and now we prefer the World Class T5 over the Corvette 4+3.

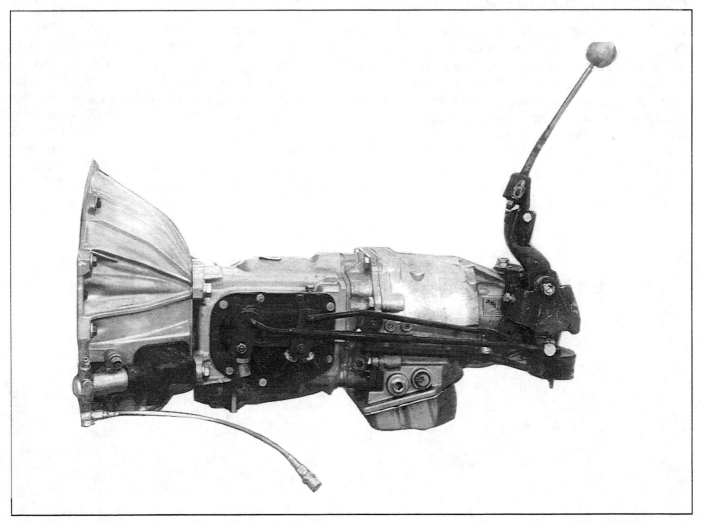

The Corvette 4+3 transmission shown above has custom made shift linkages and brackets for use in a V8 Datsun Z (Did you know that JTR has a V8 conversion manual for the 1970-1978 Datsun Z Car?) This same set-up was also used in a Jaguar XJ-S (Did you know that JTR has a V8 conversion manual for 1974-1986 Jaguars?). The shifter is a Hurst Competition Plus. The shift lever, complete with rubber bushing, is from a 1970 Datsun Z. The rubber bushing is required to cut down the noise and vibration that travel up through the shift linkage.

Custom made shift-linkages and brackets are required to install the 4+3 into most cars. In addition, the width of the overdrive unit also requires that the transmission tunnel be widened in most vehicles. Another consideration when using the 4+3 is that the driveshaft yoke only goes into the transmission about 2-5/8". A "normal" transmission will allow the yoke to go in about 3-1/2 inches. In addition, the rear mount will require custom brackets to install in most vehicles.

If you are going to install the 4+3 transmission into your vehicle, the above photo should help you with the shift linkage.

MANUAL TRANSMISSIONS

CORVETTE SIX-SPEED

The ZF six-speed transmission (used in 1989 and newer Corvettes) is an interesting, and slightly misunderstood unit. It is a very expensive transmission, and the gears rattle at engine speeds of less than 1500 rpm in sixth gear when the transmission is cold. Even with two overdrive gears (top gear is .50:1, fifth gear is .75:1), it is not at all cost effective from a fuel economy standpoint in most applications. A few mods are required to install the six-speed into some vehicles. It's more of a novelty than anything else for most people, but for those who want the strongest, slickest shifting overdrive transmission available, this is the transmission to get. We have not once heard of anybody breaking the ZF six-speed, so it must be pretty strong.

We originally had the six-speed in a V8 powered Jaguar XJ-S (Did you know...?) but we got lazy (the Jag now has a 700-R4 automatic). A common comment about the transmission was that when it was cold, it sounded a bit like a heavy-duty truck transmission. Actually, the transmission was not that noisy, but Jaguars are so quiet that many normal noises that go unnoticed in the Corvette, are quite noticeable in Jaguar. After the transmission warmed up, it would get considerably quieter.

The Corvette transmission uses a unique "Dual-Mass" flywheel to reduce the gear rattle at low engine speeds. The flywheel was actually developed to help the Corvette meet EPA fuel economy requirements. The Corvettes use a "CAGS" (Computer Aided Gear Selection) to beat the EPA gas-guzzler tax. The CAGS system, under certain conditions, blocks out second and third gears when upshifting from first gear at light throttle, forcing a first to fourth upshift. The actual shift doesn't feel that bad, and you get used to it fairly quickly, because it only happens at light throttle. In real life driving, the CAGS may not do much for fuel mileage, but in the EPA test, it allows the Corvette to beat the Gas-Guzzler tax.

O.K., so what does the "Dual-Mass" flywheel have to do with fuel economy? If a conventional flywheel was used with the six-speed gearbox and CAGS, a lot of gear rattle would be heard in fourth gear at low engine speeds. To make a long story short, and to avoid a lengthy technical explanation, the "Dual-Mass" flywheel allows the engine to run at lower speeds than normally possible, without gear rattle or engine lugging, thereby increasing fuel economy in the EPA fuel mileage test. In real world driving, the dual-mass flywheel probably helps fuel economy because it actually does promote upshifting at lower engine speeds than considered normal.

The Corvette six-speed is a much heftier unit than the T5 transmission used in the V8 Camaro. The V8 T5 is rated for 300 ft-lbs of torque, and the six-speed is (conservatively) rated for 450 ft-lbs of torque. The six-speed transmission, complete with flywheel, pressure plate, bellhousing, clutch disc, and pivot fork weighs about 205 lbs. A V8 T5 Camaro transmission, complete with TPI flywheel (16 lb nodular iron), pressure plate, bellhousing, clutch disc and pivot fork, weighs 130 lbs.

The distance between the centerlines of the transmission mainshaft and countergear has a lot to do with the strength of a transmission. (The greater the distance, the stronger the transmission.) On the six-speed, this distance is 95mm (3.74 inches), on the T5, it is 77 mm (3.03 inches). The Borg-Warner Super T-10, which was used behind big-block muscle-cars, has a mainshaft/countergear distance of 83.5 mm (3.29 inches).

The Camaro 5-speed transmission is on the left, and the Corvette six-speed is on the right. The Camaro transmission is tilted 17 degrees when installed in the Camaro. The reason for this is to offset the shifter to the driver's side. Both transmissions are shown with the shifters in the neutral position.

Note that the bolt pattern for the six-speed bellhousing is completely different from any other GM transmission.

The six-speed uses the same, 26 spline input shaft as the V8 T5, but the "deck height" (distance from the tip on the input shaft to the surface of the transmission that meets the bellhousing) is 3/8" shorter.

The output shaft of the six-speed uses the same spline as a Turbo-400 transmission. That is, a driveshaft yoke for a Turbo-400 will fit onto the six-speed.

The speedometer gear sleeve from a 700-R4 transmission also fits the six-speed.

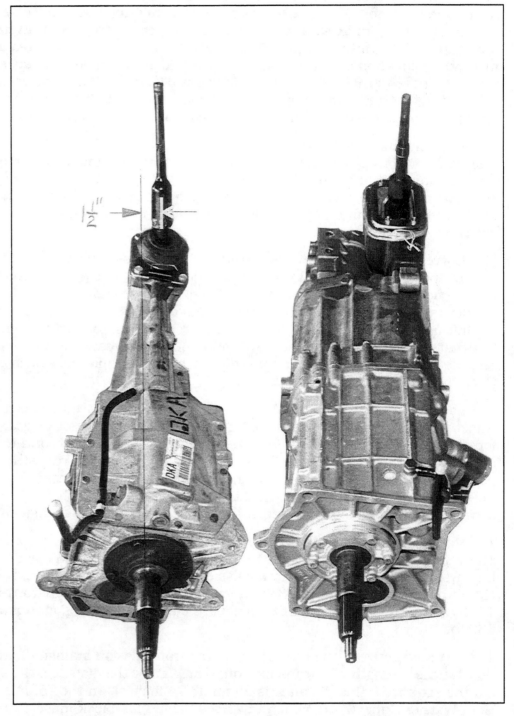

The six-speed is 1/2" shorter in length than the T5, the shifter position at the transmission is about two inches further back that the Camaro T5, and it is offset to the driver's side by about 1-3/4" more than the Camaro T5. A bracket for the rear transmission mount, which is nearly identical to the 4+3 transmission, must be fabricated for most applications.

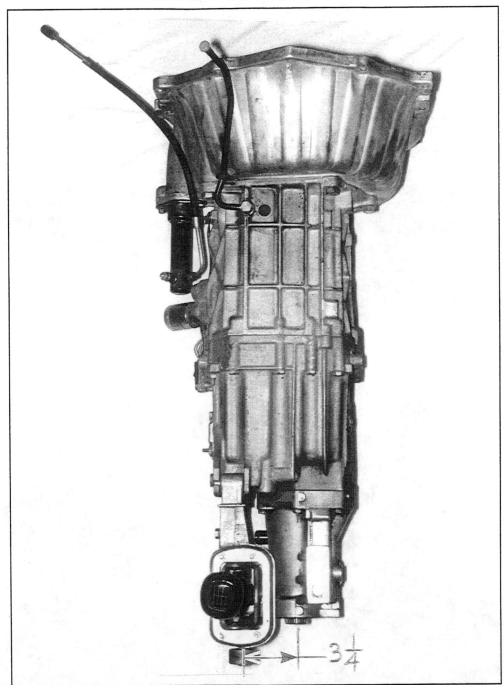

There are a few obstacles to installing the ZF six-speed into non-Corvettes. First of all, the ZF has a unique bolt pattern which requires the 1989-1992 Corvette bellhousing. This means that the only normal clutch release is going to be the stock Corvette pull-type clutch, which means that the "dual-mass" flywheel is required, which means that the engine must be 1986 or newer, with the one piece rear main seal. The Corvette set-up requires about .46 cubic inches of fluid displacement for adequate clutch disengagement.

The second obstacle is the size of the ZF transmission. The slave cylinder and "CAGS" solenoid stick out quite a bit which can interfere with transmission tunnels. Often, a little "clearance" work with a hammer will solve the slave cylinder and CAGS solenoid problems. (Hammer the transmission tunnel, not the transmission!)

One item that can solve several problems is the Tilton Hydraulic release bearing. It will effectively cure the requirement for 1986 and newer engines and the dual-mass flywheel. It will also improve transmission tunnel clearance by eliminating the Corvette slave cylinder. Not using the dual-mass flywheel may also make the transmission unbearably noisy for street driven vehicles.

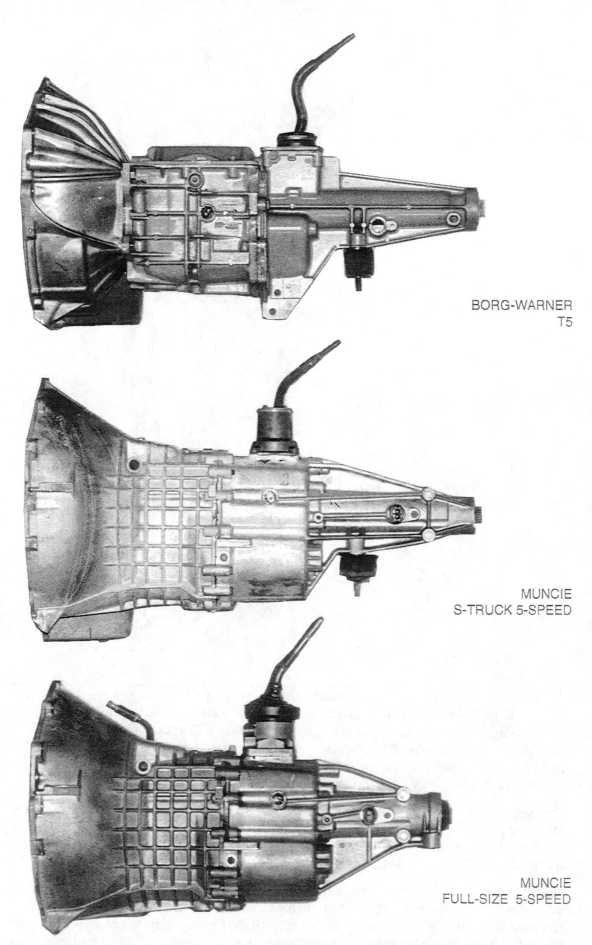

BORG-WARNER
T5

MUNCIE
S-TRUCK 5-SPEED

MUNCIE
FULL-SIZE 5-SPEED

MANUAL TRANSMISSIONS

The top transmission is a Borg-Warner T5 transmission for an S-10 truck. It is used behind the 2.8 V6, and the 2.5 four cylinder, but it is not used behind the 4.3 V6 in the S-10 Trucks (it is used behind the 4.3 V6 in the Astro vans). It is attached to a bellhousing from a full-size truck.

The center transmission is a Muncie 5-speed for an S-10 truck with the 4.3 V6.

The lower transmission is a Muncie 5-speed for a 1988-1992 1/2 ton full-size truck with engines up to the 350 TBI.

As you can see, the Borg-Warner 5-speed transmission and the Muncie 5-speed for the S-10 Truck have the same length, shifter position, rear mount position, and output shaft. The overall length and the rear mount position are the same as the 700-R4 automatic transmission.

The Muncie 5-speed for the full-size truck is shorter than the S-10 Truck transmissions, it has a different rear mount position, the output shaft is larger, and the vent tube sticks up higher. The transmission is the same length as a Turbo-400 transmission, it has the same rear mount position, and the output shaft is the same as the Turbo-400 transmission.

The biggest obstacle to installing either of the 2WD Muncies in most 2WD swaps is that there are no provisions to install a speedometer cable onto the Muncie transmissions. All 1989 and newer Chevrolet trucks use electric speedometers. Adapting an electric speedometer into a truck not already equipped can be a lot of work and cost a lot of money. The 4X4 trucks have the speedometer cable attached to the transfer case.

S-10 Trucks with the Muncie 5-speed use a damper on the differential yoke (GM part #26014374) to reduce gear rattle at low engine speeds.

The Muncie 5-speed from full-size trucks does not use a damper. We have noticed a lot of gear rattle in the "full-size" Muncie 5-speed in our S-10 Truck at engine speeds below 2000 rpm in second, third, and fourth gears, and below 1500 rpm in fifth gear; however, we have not installed a damper.

The Borg-Warner T5 weighs about 75 lbs. as shown. The Muncie 5-speed transmissions weigh about 115 lbs. as shown. The mainshaft/countergear distance on the Borg-Warner T5 transmission is 77 mm, the mainshaft/countergear distance for the Muncie transmissions is about 85 mm. The overdrive ratio on the S-10 Truck Muncie is .83:1. On the "full-size" Muncie, overdrive is .73:1.

CLUTCH RELEASE

One problem with many engine/transmission swaps is the clutch release. Hydraulic clutch release is now used on many vehicles and is more easily adaptable for engine/transmission swaps than older mechanical clutch release mechanisms.

One problem with hydraulic clutch releases is getting the clutch to release properly for good driver feel. Many times people complain about the clutch not fully releasing, even with the clutch pedal all the way to the floor. Another complaint is that the clutch pedal is too stiff, and that it behaves like an on/off switch.

The solution to the above problems is the correct combination of bellhousing, master cylinder, and slave cylinder.

Before 1984, the only Chevrolet bellhousing that used a hydraulic clutch release came on some heavy-duty trucks made in the 1960's. In 1984, Chevrolet began using hydraulic clutches on Corvettes, Camaros, and S-10 trucks. In 1988, the full-size trucks began using hydraulic clutches.

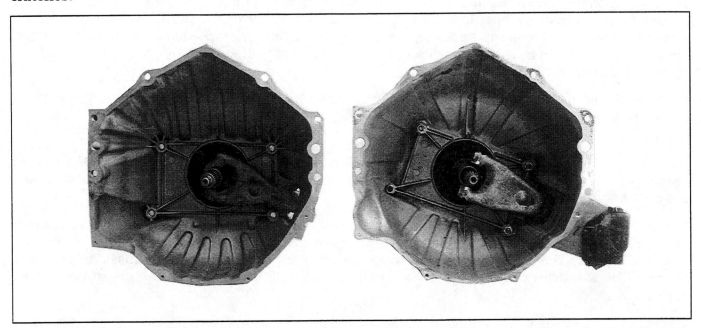

The 1984-1988 Corvette bellhousing is shown on the left and the 1984-1992 Camaro bellhousing is shown on the right. Both bellhousings use the same bolt pattern to attach the transmission. The older Muncie 4-speeds, Saginaw 4-speeds, and Borg-Warner Super T-10s will all bolt to the Corvette and Camaro bellhousings, however, the Camaro bellhousing tilts the transmission about 17 degrees for clearance reasons in the Camaro. While the Camaro T5 transmission can be bolted to the Corvette bellhousing and vice-versa; the Camaro bellhousing uses smaller, metric threads (12mm x 1.75 P) for attaching the transmission to the bellhousing compared to the standard American threads used on the Corvette. The Corvette bellhousing uses metric threads (10 mm x 1.50 P) for attaching the slave cylinder.

When using the Camaro bellhousing, the release fork sticks out quite a bit and may interfere with the transmission tunnel. A little "hammer work" will often solve minor clearance problems. Often, the "hammer work" can cause the transmission tunnel to get in the way of the throttle pedal, so the gas pedal should be checked to make sure it doesn't stick to the floor.

The clutch slave cylinder used on the 1984-1988 Corvette is made by Girling and has a 1.0" bore. Girling (available from Tilton Engineering) has other slave cylinders with different bore diameters that will bolt to the Corvette bellhousing. With the 1.0" bore, the slave cylinder requires .55 cubic inches of fluid displacement to adequately release the 10-1/2" diaphragm clutch that is used on the 1984-1988 Corvettes.

A 7/8" bore slave cylinder (available from Tilton Engineering) reduces the fluid displacement to .43 cubic inches, which is more in line with other vehicle's hydraulic clutch requirements.

CAMARO SLAVE CYLINDER MODIFICATIONS

Some simple modifications can be done to the Camaro slave cylinder to attach the hydraulic line to a non-Camaro master cylinder. The Camaro slave cylinder uses a roll pin to secure the hydraulic hose (which is made of plastic). Sealing is accomplished with a rubber o-ring. Unfortunately, we have not been able to find a simple way to connect conventional flare fittings to the Camaro's plastic slave cylinder, or connect the plastic hose to non-Camaro slave cylinders.

We have successfully used the following procedure to adapt the Camaro slave cylinder to more conventional hydraulic hose fittings.

1. Disassemble the slave cylinder by removing the retaining clip and removing the piston, seals and spring.
2. Use a hacksaw and cut the plastic housing where the hydraulic hose is attached so that it is about 1/8" taller than the bleed screw boss.
3. Drill and tap the housing for a 1/8" pipe thread.
4. Thoroughly clean out all of the plastic filings and other debris.
5. Re-assemble the slave cylinder.
6. Install the slave cylinder on the bellhousing.
7. Use the fittings as shown to attach the hydraulic hose to the slave cylinder. Use teflon tape on all connections and be careful not to over-tighten the pipe nipple going into the slave cylinder.

See photo on following page.

Clutch parts as shown:

1. 3/16" (–3, or dash 3) braided hose.

2. Adapter. 1/8" pipe to –3 hose.

3. 1/8" pipe coupler.

4. 1/8" pipe nipple, 1-1/2" long.

Another solution would be to install the slave cylinder from an S-10 truck or a full-size truck onto the Camaro bellhousing with an adapter plate to properly install and orient the slave cylinder. The truck slave cylinders are made of steel, and use flare fittings for the hydraulic connections.

The Camaro slave cylinder requires about .45 cubic inches of fluid displacement to properly release the 10-1/2 diaphragm clutch that is used on V8 Camaros.

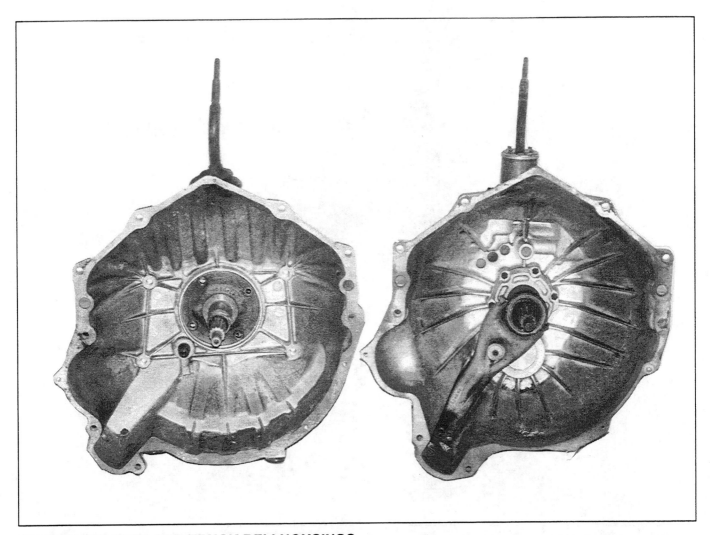

CLUTCH RELEASE AND TRUCK BELLHOUSINGS

On the left is a Borg-Warner T5 attached to a bellhousing from a 1988-1992 full-size truck (GM part #15562385, cost ~$160). A pilot ring (5.125" o.d. by 4.686" i.d.) can be made to properly center the transmission into the full-size truck bellhousing.

On the right is a Muncie 5-speed that is used in the 1990 and newer 4.3 V6 S-10 Trucks.

There is a slight difference in the position of the slave cylinder between the two transmissions, which is done for clearance reasons between the bellhousing and the frame on the S-10 Truck.

When used with the full-size slave cylinder and an 11 inch diaphragm clutch, the master cylinder must displace about .50 cubic inches of hydraulic fluid for adequate clutch disengagement. When used with a 10-1/2" diaphragm clutch, the master cylinder must displace about .43 cubic inches of hydraulic fluid for adequate clutch release. The numbers for adequate clutch release are based on .38 inches of movement at the throwout bearing for the 10-1/2" diaphragm clutch, and .44 inches of movement at the throwout bearing for the 11" diaphragm clutch.

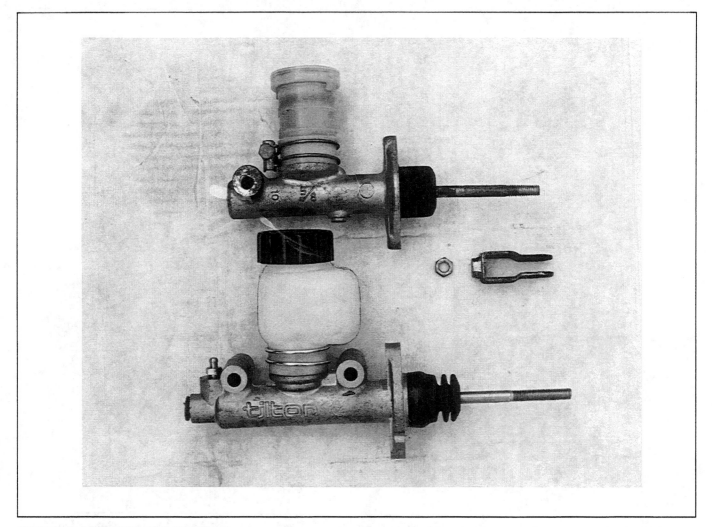

CLUTCH MASTER CYLINDERS

The upper master cylinder is used in a Datsun 240 Z. It has a 5/8" bore diameter and is 4-1/2" long when measured from the mounting flange. The master cylinder on the bottom is made by Tilton Engineering (805-688-2353). It is 5-1/2" long and is available in eight different bore diameters ranging from 5/8" to 1-1/8". It can literally be bolted into the Datsun, Volvos, and many other cars. AP-Lockheed also makes several styles of master cylinders, one of which is an extra short model that is only 3-1/4" long. One potential problem with the extra short model is that the stroke is only 1", compared to 1.2" for the Tilton unit. The shorter stroke may not displace enough fluid for adequate clutch release in some applications. A large number of different master cylinders are used in various original equipment applications, and a lot of them use common mounting provisions.

When installing a manual transmission with a hydraulic clutch, it is important that the master cylinder is compatible in fluid displacement with the slave cylinder requirements for proper clutch release. If you cannot find a factory master cylinder to work with your engine swap, the aftermarket master cylinders may solve your clutch release problems. Many race car fabrication shops carry Tilton Engineering and AP-Lockheed parts.

WIRING

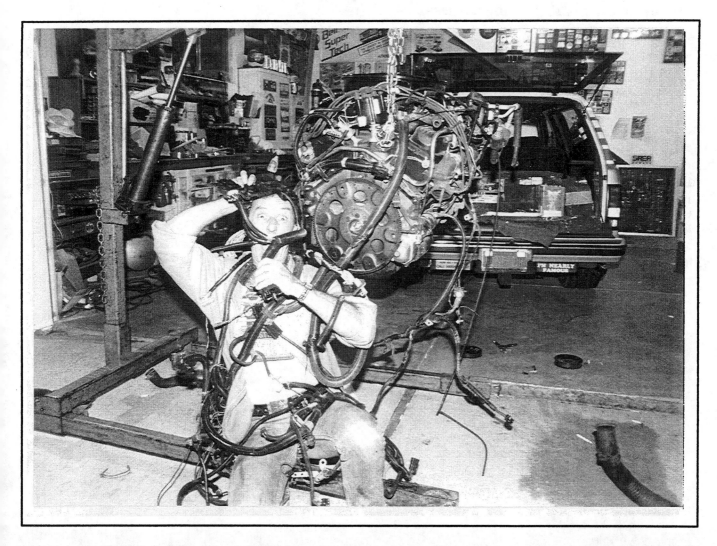

The *nearly* famous pinstriper, Herb Martinez, (aka, The Line Doctor) installed a 305 TBI V8 into his 2WD S-15 Jimmy using the factory wiring harness. Herbie was so traumatized by the "WIRE MONSTER" that he could not pull a straight paint line for weeks. Thankfully, Herb has fully recovered, and is again the best pinstriper in the business. You can see his work on a lot of show cars, and on cars featured in magazines.

The "wiring experience" does not have to be an awful experience, but if your are not familiar with wiring, it probably will be an awful experience. The factory fuel-injection wiring harness can be controlled, routed, and installed into most vehicles. However, if this your first experience, be prepared for a generous amount of swearing, frustration, and confusion. You should probably plan on spending over 50 hours to study the shop manual, label the wires, understand what you are doing, connect the wires, and clean up the mess.

It's not an easy job, but you will have more confidence and understanding of the entire fuel-injection system if you use the factory wiring harness.

WIRING HARNESSES—FACTORY OR AFTERMARKET?

There are two ways to wire the fuel injected engines: You can use the factory wiring harness, or you can buy an aftermarket wiring harness.

In previous editions of this manual, we did not recommend using aftermarket harnesses because they were all simplified too much. Since this book has been in print (or because this book has been in print), some aftermarket wiring harnesses have improved, but some are still too simple.

USING THE FACTORY WIRING HARNESS IS VERY TIME CONSUMING

In the first edition of this manual, we assumed that people purchased this book because they wanted to reduce the cost of their conversion by using the factory wiring harness. We later learned that many people just plain don't want to deal with wiring and wiring schematics. Using the factory wiring harness in a fuel-injected engine swap generally takes the first-timer at least 50 hours because of the studying and learning required.

If you decide to buy an aftermarket wiring harness to work with the stock GM computer, make sure it is designed to be used with a Vehicle Speed Sensor (VSS), because without a VSS, the engine will not function the way GM engineers designed it to run.

WIRING

USING THE FACTORY WIRING HARNESS

As mentioned in the chapter on buying engines, when you get your engine, it should have a complete harness. If the harness is damaged, and cannot be salvaged, the replacement cost for the Camaro harness is not that bad (under $300), but for a Corvette, it is that bad (about $750)!

Rule #1: Use the factory shop manual for your engine (available from Helm (800)782-4356) and label all unconnected wires and connectors on the wiring harness *BEFORE* you change anything on the engine. Also, label all unconnected wires and connectors *BEFORE* you install the engine.

Many people want to simplify and streamline the factory harness for easier installation.

We at JTR ask the question: Don't you think the engineers and bean counters at General Motors designed the factory wiring harness to be as reliable and <u>inexpensive</u> as possible?

There are not that many wires that can be removed from the factory harness while still keeping the engine fully functional as GM designed it. Some wires can be removed from the harness such as the wiring for windshield wipers and washer, and the electric cooling fan wiring can be removed if other fan switches and controls are installed. On non-pollution controlled vehicles, the wiring for the AIR injection and evaporative emissions canister can be removed. But that is really about all of the wiring that can be removed. If the EGR wiring is removed, the engine will not run properly and the "Check Engine" light will go on.

The factory harness can also be modified by rerouting wires, shortening wires, and extending wires. Properly done, this can make the harness look simpler and less cluttered.ADVANTAGES OF THE FACTORY WIRING HARNESS

The nice thing about using the factory harness is that there is complete documentation in the GM Service Manuals (available from Helm) to label the harness, and to troubleshoot the wiring if there should ever be a problem. The other nice thing about using the factory harness is that it is complete with *all* wiring for the engine; this includes wiring for the gauges, starter, alternator, electric cooling fans (if applicable), air-conditioning, and even power to the fuse box.

The point is: If you want to install a TPI or TBI engine into your vehicle and you want the emissions controls, air-conditioning, electric cooling fan, and lock-up torque converter fully integrated with the ECM (Engine Control Module), and you want the wiring for the instrument panel, and power to the fuse box, alternator, starter, and ignition combined into the wiring harness... using the factory wiring harness may be simpler than trying to add everything to a simplified harness.

Another reason we like the factory harness is for environmental protection. The factory harness has safeguards against corrosion. All the splices are crimped and soldered. All the connectors in the engine compartment are water resistant, the harness is configured (routed) to prevent heat damage, and the harness is designed to allow for engine movement.

Yet another reason we prefer the factory harness is that the color codes of the wires will exactly match the color codes in the shop manual (Available from Helm) which makes any trouble shooting far easier than trying to guess which wire goes to the problem area.

If you have read this far, you can probabley understand the advantages of using the factory engine wiring harness with all of the appropriate sensors when installing a fuel-injected engine into your vehicle. Chevrolet engineers are not stupid, and they did not add extra wires and sensors for the fun of it. The wiring and sensors are there for reasons of drivability, reliability, emissions, and safety.

The first thing you should know about *wiring* is that there is a lot more to wiring than simply connecting wires. It consists of *routing* wires, *mounting* relays and electronic modules, making sure that the wiring *does not get melted* by exhaust heat, and making sure that the wiring *will not get torn* by engine movement.

WIRING

Connecting wires scares a lot of brave people, especially when it comes time to hook up the battery cables. Simply put, connecting wires is like the dot-to-dot games you played in grammar school. The big difference is that you have to *label* the wires yourself (both on the engine's wiring harness and the chassis' wiring harness) before you connect the dots (or wires).

Labeling the wires requires the shop manual for the vehicle that the engine came out of, and the shop manual for the vehicle that the engine is going into. You have to buy the shop manuals because they will be your only guide. Even if the shop manuals cost $100 each (and some do), they will quickly pay for themselves with the amount of time they will save you.

The best shop manual for labeling the fuel-injection wiring is the factory shop manual available from Helm. If you buy some other brand of shop manual or wiring guide, you will suffer much difficulty with labeling and connecting wires.

USE THE FACTORY SHOP MANUALS AVAILABLE FROM HELM!
Their phone number is (800)782-4356

At this point, this must be stated: If you don't understand the basics of fuel-injection and wiring, you can learn. If you won't **study** the factory shop manuals, you should not be doing the TPI/TBI engine swap because you will never have complete confidence in the system if a minor problem occurs and you don't know how to fix it. A good engine swap is one that you feel confident of driving anywhere, and not fearing that it will require a specialist should it need repair. As stated earlier, this manual is a supplement to the factory shop manuals, and will cover information that is not covered in the factory shop manuals.

Most likely, your first experience with wiring any of the fuel-injected engines will be frustrating, confusing, and time consuming. After you successfully do your first TPI/TBI engine swap, the next one (nobody does just one!) will be much easier because you will have the experience of using the factory shop manual and you will be comfortable with having to look things up in the shop manual.

COMMON QUESTIONS

The most commonly asked question by people installing fuel-injected engines into their previously non-fuel-injected engines is:

"Can I install different dash gauges in my vehicle without affecting the ECM?"

The answer is:

"Yes, you can install different gauges. The only thing the ECM controls on the dash is the 'Check Engine' light. On 1990 and newer Corvettes and TPI Camaros, the ECM sends signals to the electric speedometer, the cruise control, and the radio volume (Corvettes only), but the computer (ECM) is not affected if the wires for the cruise control, electric speedometer, and radio are not connected to anything."

The most common misconception of the fuel-injected engines is that the instrument panel is operated by the engine computer (ECM). This is absolutely not true. The instrument gauges (oil pressure, water temperature, tachometer, voltmeter, fuel gauge, etc.) are not connected to, or controlled by the ECM. The wires for the instruments are in the engine wiring harness, but they are not connected to the ECM. So if you want to change the oil pressure sending unit and the water temperature sending unit to match your gauges, go ahead, this will not affect the fuel-injection.

The "Check Engine" light or "Service Engine Soon" (SES) light, which is on the instrument panel, is controlled by the ECM. The "Check Engine" light will go on for various reasons, including overheating and overcharging, but the ECM gets this information from engine sensors that are in no way connected to the gauges on the instrument panel.

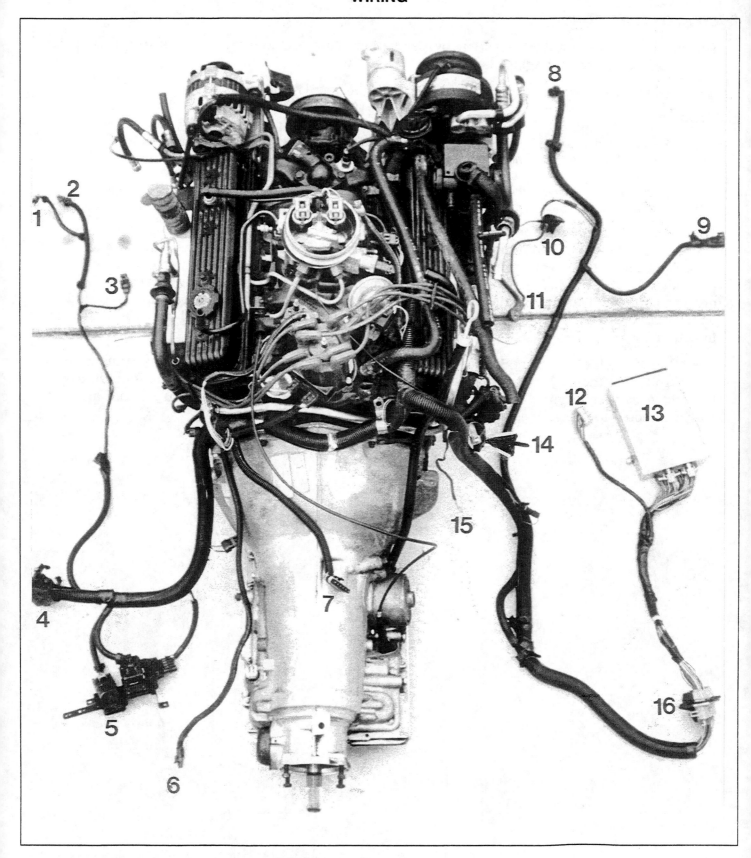

1988 CAMARO 305 TBI V-8 ENGINE AND 700-R4 TRANSMISSION

1989–1992 Camaro 305 TBI engines are similar.

WIRING

To the left is a 1988 305 TBI engine and transmission, as pulled from a wrecked Camaro (the transmission output shaft has been replaced with a 4X4 output shaft). This engine & transmission went into a S-10 4X4 Blazer.

The wiring harness has the following items labeled.

1. Charcoal canister.
2. Power steering pressure switch.
3. Windshield washer bottle.
4. Bulkhead connector.
5. Relays and ESC (Electronic Spark Control).
6. Electric speedometer.
7. Camaro windshield wiper motor.
8. Electric cooling fan.
9. Fuse for ECM.
10. Junction block.
11. Positive battery cable.
12. 15-pin connector.
13. ECM.
14. Air conditioning, high speed blower, and MAP (Manifold Air Pressure) sensor.
15. Ground strap. Bolts to firewall
16. Firewall bulkhead grommet.

The only real wiring is on items 4 (bulkhead connector) and 12 (15-pin connector). The other parts of the wiring harness are either plugged into a mating part, bolted down to something, or removed from the harness. Some of the wiring will probably be rerouted, shortened, or extended.

Don't be afraid to pull the loom (plastic covering) off the harness to trace wires. A good technique is to secure the harness with electrical tape every 10 inches, to keep it from going everywhere when the covering is removed.

Remember, this harness has wiring for everything from the instruments, air conditioning, power distribution wires, alternator, and battery cables, just like a carbureted engine, and all of it is compatible with most 1970 and newer GM cars. A simplified fuel-injection wiring harness would not include these wires, which is why they can be made so simply.

This is a 1988 305 TPI engine just after it was removed from a Firebird. The engine is complete from the air-cleaner and ducting to the charcoal canister and purge valves. Even the in-tank fuel-pump (not shown) and the exhaust system were supplied with the engine. The wiring harness is also complete—from the electronic control unit (ECM) to the battery cables, and even the spark plug wires. The engine was removed without damaging a single wire.

This is the proper way to receive the engine. Trying to do an engine swap with parts missing from the engine or damaged wiring will turn the fuel-injected V8 conversion process into a costly, time consuming, and frustrating experience.

WIRING

This engine was purchased from GM Sports Salvage, which specializes in Camaros and Firebirds. They are in San Jose, California (408) 432-8498 and have the best selection of Camaro/Firebird engines and transmissions in our area.

1. Fuse (ECM memory)

2. Windshield washer pump

3. Negative battery cable

4. Positive battery cable

5. Relays and ESC

6. Bulkhead connector

7. Windshield wiper motor

8. Throttle cable

9. Reverse switch for back-up light (manual transmission only) or for torque converter lock-up (automatic transmissions)

10. Electrical speedometer

11. Wiring and relays for cooling fans

12. A.C. fan pressure switch

13. A.C. and high speed blower connector

14. 15-pin connector

15. ECM

16. Firewall bulkhead grommet

The wiring harness for a pre-1988 TPI Camaro/Firebird engine is different, but a lot of the layout is the same as the 1988 engine that is shown.

Again, the factory shop manual (available from Helm at 1-800-782-4356) will have all the information required for you to label the wires.

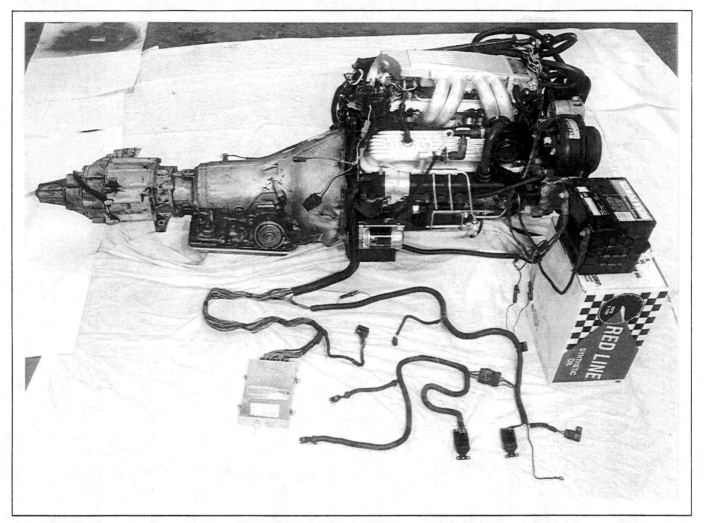

One reason many people are afraid of the stock wiring harness is because of all the "extra" wires on the engine harness. A lot of the "extra" wiring consists of wiring for the electric cooling fans and fan control switches and relays. The air conditioning wiring also adds to the complexity.

This 1989 350 TPI engine/700-R4 transmission/New Process transfer case is going into an S-10 Blazer 4X4, and the wiring is mocked up to insure that we know where everything will connect before it is installed. Notice that even the battery cables are connected to a battery.

On the next page, the wiring for the electric cooling fans and the air conditioning fan control switch has been erased from the photo. Notice how much simpler the wiring harness looks.

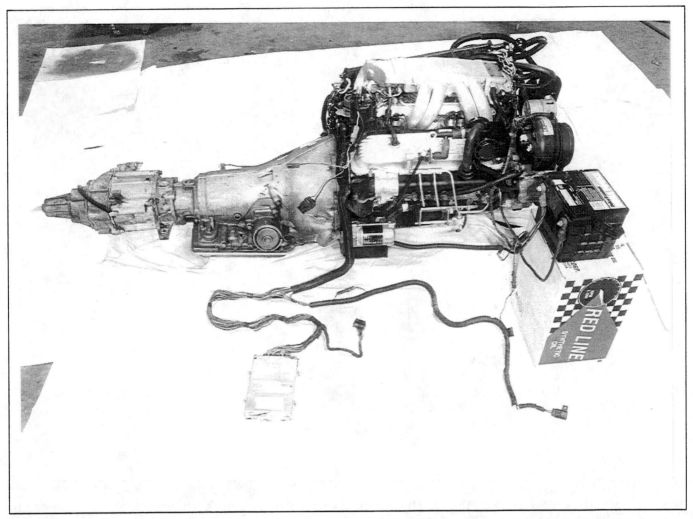

Notice how much simpler the harness looks with just a few snips of the wire cutters (or a few strokes of White-Out™). Only the wiring for the electric cooling fans was removed for this illustration.

Also notice how everything on the harness is connected to something and serves a purpose. There are not a lot of "extra" wires used on the factory harness.

This is the wiring with fuel-injection components on a 1989 350 TPI engine/700-R4 transmission ready to go into an S-10 4X4 Blazer. The wiring harness has been modified slightly by relocating the wiring for the MAF sensor and charcoal canister, and removing the wiring for the windshield wipers and electric speedometer.

Notice that there are "only" eleven wires to connect to the vehicle on this side of the Camaro harness. These go to the instruments, the fuse box, the ignition switch, and the brake pedal switch (for the lock-up torque converter). Everything else *plugs* into a component such as the relays, charcoal canister, MAF sensor, and ESC (electronic spark control) module. The relays, charcoal canister, and ESC module are simply bolted down wherever its convenient.

The 11 wires go to:

1&2. Two wires are power for the fuse box.

3. Starter motor.

4. Ignition coil

5. Water temperature sending unit.

6. Oil pressure sending unit.

7. Torque converter clutch (from the brake pedal switch).

8. Power to emission controls.

9. Fuel pump.

10. Alternator.

11. Tachometer.

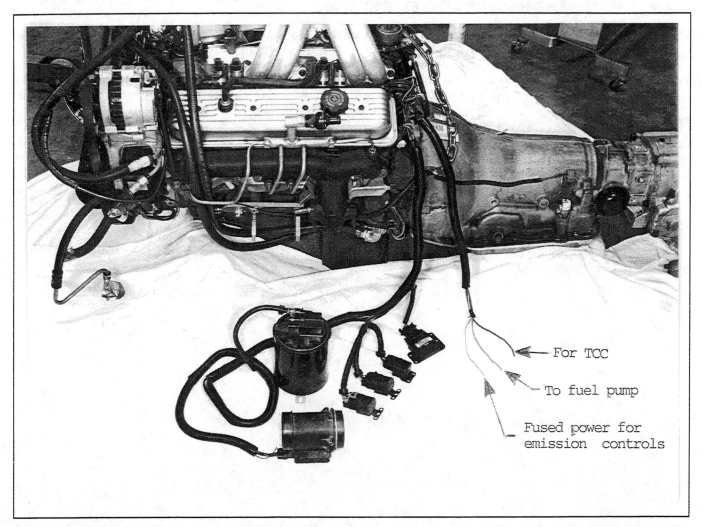

For TCC

To fuel pump

Fused power for
emission controls

If the wiring not connected to the ECM is eliminated from the harness, the actual wiring for the fuel-injection looks a lot simpler. Only three "stray" wires need to be connected to the vehicle on this side of the 1989 Camaro engine wiring harness.

The wiring for the water temperature sending unit, oil pressure sending unit, alternator, fuse box, ignition coil, starter solenoid, and tachometer are independent of the fuel-injection, and are used the same as with a carbureted engine. While it is true that the wiring listed on the previous page is in the "engine wiring harness," it is not *connected* to any wiring for the fuel-injection part of the harness, except for the three wires labeled above.

If you want to change the oil pressure sending unit and the water temperature sending unit to match the instruments in your vehicle, go ahead, it will not affect the fuel-injection. We feel this point bears repeating because it is one of the most asked questions about wiring the fuel-injected engines.

WIRING TIPS FOR THE 1990-1991 CORVETTE ENGINES

1990-1991 Corvettes use a Central Control Module (CCM), which receives information from the ECM, the heater/air-conditioner module, and the brake control module.

There are two circuit #800 wires on the 1990-1991 Corvette ECM (Cavity R11 and R5) which are wired to the CCM and to the brake control module and to the heater/air-conditioner module at splice S222.

The 1990-1991 Corvette engine/transmission will work fine without the ECM wiring being connected to the CCM, or to the heater/air-conditioner module, or to the brake control module. The ECM sends information to the CCM, but the CCM does not send information to the ECM.

The ECM is wired to the ALDL (Assembly Line Diagnostics Link) by splicing the two circuit #800 wires together and connecting them to cavity M of the ALDL.

Other than the above, the wiring for the 1990-1991 Corvette engine/transmission is straightforward, *but very tedious.*l

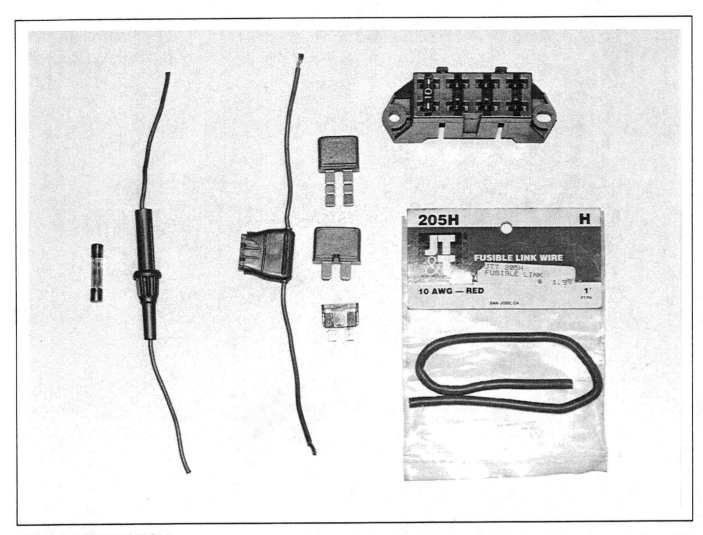

WIRING PROTECTION

In case a circuit gets "shorted," the factory uses protection in the form of fuses, fusible links, and circuit breakers as shown above. These components should be installed wherever they are shown in the factory shop manual.

These parts are available at most auto parts stores, and at your Chevrolet dealership.

We prefer the ATO (blade) type of fuse over the glass type of fuse because it is easier to see if they are broken, and because they have fewer "poor connection" problems.

RELAYS

Relays are often used to allow a low amperage switch to control a high amperage circuit. For example, many non-GM cars use a relay to supply current to a starter solenoid.

It is often easier to install a relay than to install a separate switch

We have seen engines that would not start because the power to the ECM was taken from the ignition switch. Installing a relay that was activated by the ignition switch solved the problem.

The relay on the left is a *dual pole* relay. It has five terminals.

The relay on the right is a *single pole* relay. It has four terminals.

A dual pole relay is used to open or close a circuit when a switch is turned on. We often use the dual pole relay for the torque converter clutch (TCC) by connecting it to the brake pedal switch so that the TCC is turned off when the brake lights are turned on. It is wired as shown.

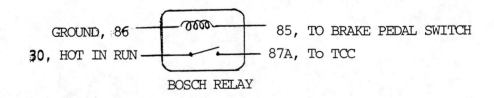

GROUND, 86   85, TO BRAKE PEDAL SWITCH

30, HOT IN RUN   87A, To TCC

BOSCH RELAY

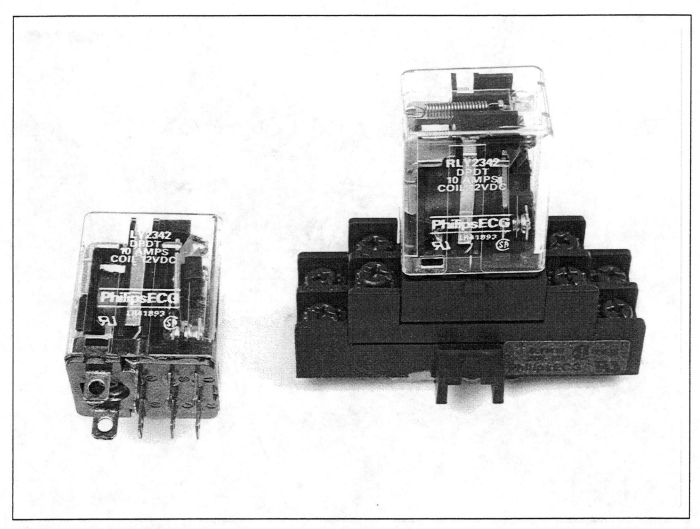

RELAYS AND SOCKETS

Dual pole, dual throw relays are shown above. The relay on the right is in a "socket," which makes it easy to connect wires with screw connectors.

We use this type of relay to operate two separate circuits from one switch, when it is difficult to install another switch. For example, we use the above relay to operate the park/neutral (P/N) circuit for the starter interlock and the P/N circuit for the ECM with a *single* P/N switch.

Wire the relays so that you do not cause a voltage spike to the ECM for the P/N switch. That is, don't wire the P/N switch so that the wires going to the ECM run through the coil of the relay. The schematics are found on the relays.

When purchasing a relay, it is important that the relay can operate continuously, and that it operates on 12 volts. Make sure that the relay can handle the amperage requirements of the circuit. Relays can be purchased at electronics stores and well stocked auto parts stores. To find one near you, look in the Yellow Pages under "Electronic equipment and supplies."

REROUTING THE WIRING

This is a 1988 Camaro TPI engine that will be installed into a Jaguar sedan. On the Camaro TPI engine, the wiring to the starter motor, knock sensor, fan switch, and fusible links are routed along the valve cover to the front of the motor and then to the back to starter, knock sensor and fan switch. However, with the "center dump" or "rams horn" exhaust manifolds, it was feared that the heat from the manifold outlet would damage the wiring. The wiring was rerouted to come in from the rear of the engine, and avoid being near the manifold outlet.

After the wiring was rerouted, some wires were shortened by cutting and soldering, other wires were extended. Extending the wires has been a point of controversy among some "experts" in the automotive field. These experts claim that lengthening a wire can cause malfunctions due to increased electrical resistance. The technical department at JTR has an inside tip: Many of these "experts" aren't really experts! A typical electrical sending unit has a resistance of anywhere between 100 ohms and 10,000 ohms. If you add a two foot length of wire, and solder the connections, the resistance under the worst conditions (we are talking about terrible solder joints) will be less than 1 ohm. 1 ohm added to a 100 ohm circuit is insignificant in automotive electrical systems. Besides, you can see we have late model computer controlled engines in our vehicles, and they work pretty well in spite of what some "experts" have told us about modifying the wiring harness. It is important to use the proper gauge wire when extending wires. We *have* seen problems caused by extending wires with thinner gauge wire.

The rerouting of the harness could have been eliminated with the use of the heat insulating tapes now on the market, but at the time of this installation, the heat insulation tapes were not readily available.

P/N (Park/Neutral) SWITCH

Some of the simplified wiring harnesses for the TPI/TBI engines ground the P/N wire so that the ECM always thinks the car is in neutral or park. The reason they do this is to prevent the SES (Service Engine Soon) light from being turned on because of the lack of a VSS.

The Chevrolet Camaro, Corvette, S-Truck, full size truck, Caprice, and Van service manuals all state:

> "The ECM uses the P/N signal as one of the inputs to control:
>
> > Idle air control
> > VSS diagnostics
> > EGR
>
> If [the P/N wire is grounded], while in drive range, the EGR would be inoperative, resulting in possible detonation."

As stated earlier, beware of harnesses that don't use a vehicle speed sensor.

If your vehicle has only one park/neutral switch, a relay can be attached to the wiring so that the original park/neutral switch will control two circuits, or another switch can be added to the shifter. If you cannot add a switch or relay, don't connect the P/N wire to anything. The car will run perfectly fine in gear, and when in park or neutral, it will also run fine, but when shifting into gear, the engine speed may momentarily drop excessively, although in our own experiences, the engines have not stalled.

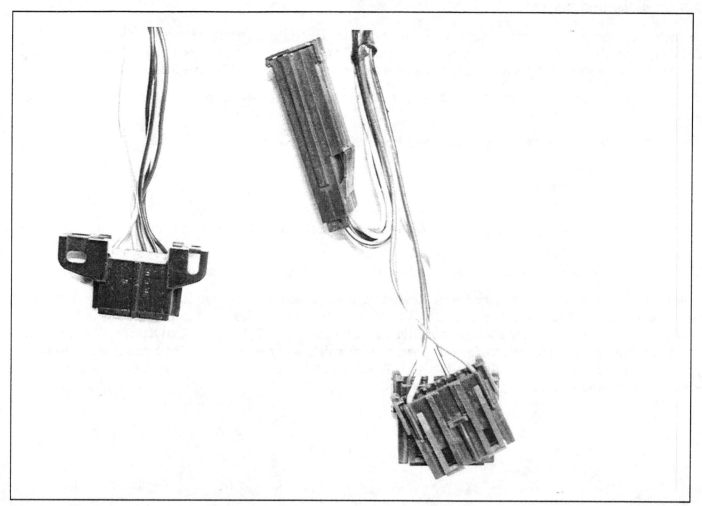

This is all the relevant wiring under the dash of a stock, 1984 V-6, automatic transmission 4X4 S-Truck, which is typical of the under-dash wiring for a computer controlled carbureted engine.

On the left is the ALDL (Assembly Line Diagnostics Link) connector. Upper center is the lamp driver module for the "check engine light" or "Service Engine Soon" (SES) light. Fuel-injected engines do not use the lamp driver module, it is incorporated into the ECM, so the lamp driver module in a computer controlled carbureted vehicle will be discarded. On the lower right is the 15-pin connector (C-207 in the Camaro manual) that will be modified to work with the Camaro/Firebird engine wiring harness.

Most of the custom wiring required to install the Camaro/Firebird engine into another vehicle is in the 15-pin connector. Of the 13 wires that go to the Camaro/Firebird 15-pin connector, 5 wires are "fused" power wires that can be "tapped" from the ignition switch. 6 wires from the 15-pin connector go to the ALDL connector. Other wires go to the vehicle speed sensor (VSS), "Service Engine Soon" (SES) or "Check Engine" light, park/neutral (P/N) switch (automatic transmission only), torque converter clutch (TCC) (automatic transmission) or shift light (manual transmission), and ground wires.

If you notice that the above list accounts for more than 13 wires, it is because wires for the TCC, grounds, and SES go to both the ALDL and the dash. The wiring sounds simple, but it can be tedious to verify all the wires for your application.

KNOCK SENSOR

On some engine swaps, the knock sensor may have to be relocated for clearance reasons.

The knock sensor responds to sounds in the knock frequency (1-3 KHZ), and sends signals to the electronic spark control (ESC) module so that the timing can be retarded to suppress harmful detonation. Because the knocking sound travels through steel and iron quite well, it can be mounted on the motor mount (as shown) with little effect on its operation. Because the knock sensor sends electrical signals to the ESC, it must have a good ground to the engine. Before installing the motor mount to the engine, remove any paint on the engine and motor mount that would prevent a good ground path for the knock sensor.

The engine shown is a 1988 350 TPI that is prepared for installation into a 4X4 S-10 truck.

Generally, we try to leave all sensors, controls and wiring as close as possible to their original configuration to ease maintenance and repairs. This way, most repairs can be done using the shop manual for the vehicle that the engine originally came from.

Knock sensors and modules are specifically tuned/calibrated for their application. Do not mix knock sensors and modules from different engines!

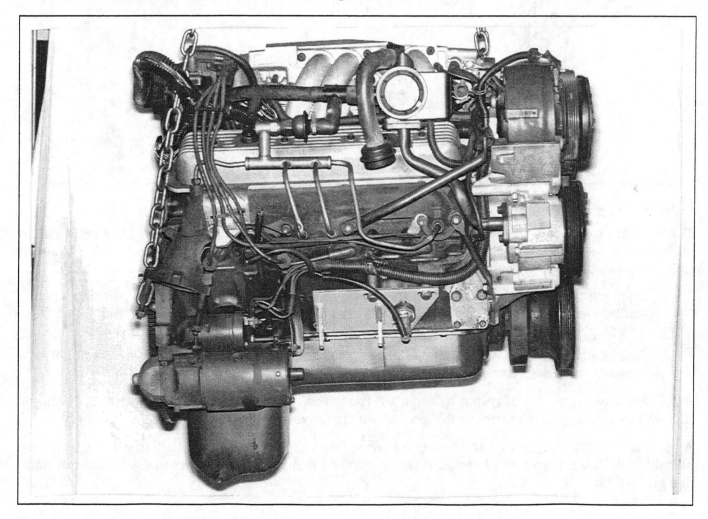

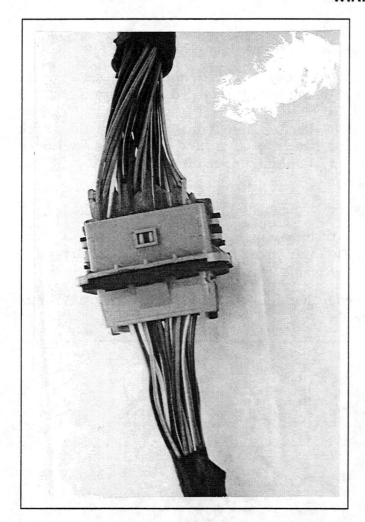
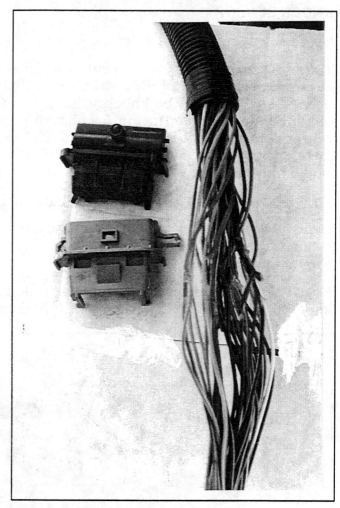

FIREWALL BULKHEAD GROMMET

The Firewall bulkhead grommet must usually be removed from the Camaro and Corvette engine wiring harness to allow the harness to be routed through the firewall with only a 2" diameter hole. This is not an easy task, but it needs to be done! Use the following procedure:

1. Undo the plastic latches and remove the plastic pieces from the harness. Use a pair of bladed screwdrivers to help pry the halves apart. You will be left with a bundle of wires that is encapsulated in a rubbery, gluey resin.

2. Carefully separate the wires from the rubbery, gluey substance. (Use a blow dryer to warm the assembly to make it easier.)

After about ten minutes of trying to separate the wires, you will be saying to yourself, "I should just go out and buy one of those aftermarket wiring harnesses."

After another 10-20 minutes of hard labor, sore fingers, and foul language, the wiring harness should look like the second photo, and you should be congratulating yourself if you did not damage any wires.

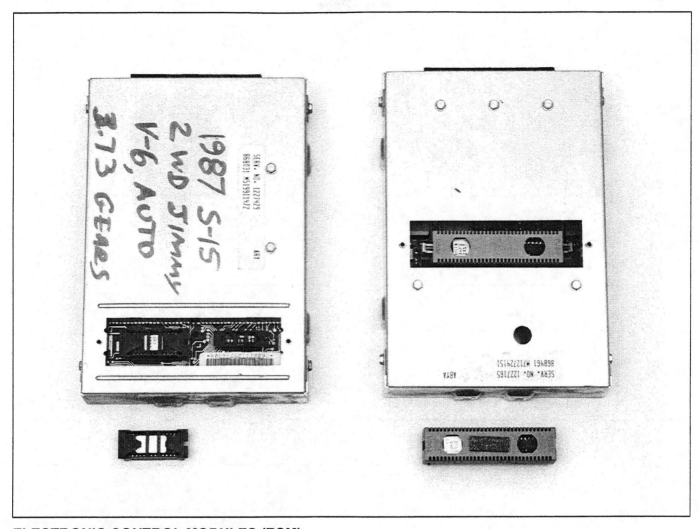

ELECTRONIC CONTROL MODULES (ECM)

On the left is a typical TBI ECM, on the right is an ECM for 1986–1989 TPI engines. Notice that they are both the same size. Some of the earlier ECMs for carbureted engines are slightly smaller.

The PROMs (or programmable chips) of both ECMs are shown below each ECM. The PROM from a TPI ECM is easy to remove, requiring little force. The TPI PROM includes the CALPAC. The PROM from a TBI ECM is more difficult to remove, requiring a bit of force. The circuit board may get damaged if you are not careful. *(The above photo shows the PROM chips both installed and extracted.)*

TBI ECMs rarely have problems, unless the circuit board gets cracked from a PROM change. 1985–1989 TPI ECMs are not as reliable. When an ECM fails, however, it rarely causes a non-running condition. Typical ECM failures result in minor drivability problems—rough idle and stalling.

The 1990 and newer TPI ECMs are reported to be much more reliable than the 1985-1989 TPI ECMs.

WIRING
Note Page

VEHICLE ANTI-THEFT SYSTEM

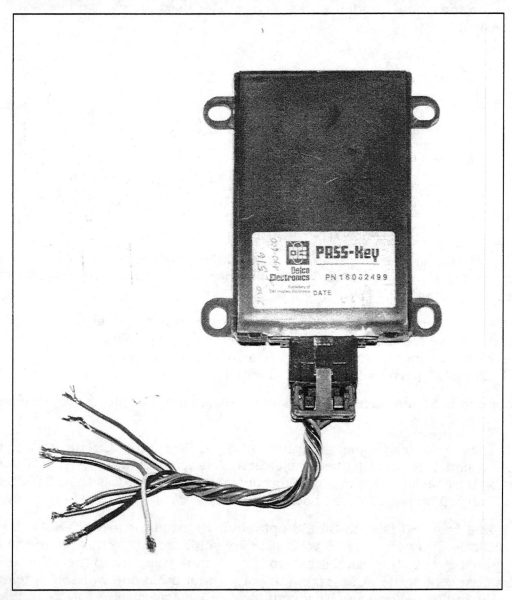

VATS (Vehicle Anti-Theft System)

1986-1991 Corvettes and 1989-1992 Camaros are equipped with VATS (also called PASS-Key).

A car equipped with VATS has a key that contains a resistor that is coded to the VATS module. A vehicle equipped with VATS will not start if an incorrect ignition key is used by disabling the starter and the injectors.

Basically, 15 differently coded keys make it difficult for car thieves to drive off in a VATS equipped vehicle. When the VATS has the correct key, it puts out a signal to the ECM, which will allow the engine to start. The signal is a 0-5 Volt, 30 Hz square wave with a 50% duty cycle.

If the wrong ignition key is used, the car will not start. There is a timer in the VATS so that even if the correct ignition key is immediately used after the wrong key was used, the car will not start for up to four minutes.

VEHICLE ANTI-THEFT SYSTEM

If you want to use the factory VATS or PASS-KEY module, and you have the patience, you can try each resistance on the module until it works. The resistor used in any given keys will have one of the following resistances.

1.	400 Ω	9.	3,025 Ω
2.	525 Ω	10.	3,730 Ω
3.	680 Ω	11.	4,750 Ω
4.	885 Ω	12.	6,050 Ω
5.	1,130 Ω	13.	7,500 Ω
6.	1,465 Ω	14.	9,540 Ω
7.	1,860 Ω	15.	11,790 Ω
8.	2,360 Ω		

The service department at Chevrolet has a tool called the "interrogator" that is used to determine the proper key code for the VATS module. Its operation is explained in the factory shop manual available from Helm (800-782-4356).

Another option is to purchase a new PASS-KEY module from the dealer. The new module will accept any of the above resistances the first time power is applied, and "burn it into memory". If you need the wiring connector (or pigtail) it is available as GM part# 12048346 (connector, 1 required) and 12020757 (terminal connector, 9 required).

Still another option is to purchase an aftermarket PROM chip that has the VATS eliminated from its program.

If you want to make your own signal generator, a 555 IC (Integrated Circuit) can be used to produce the proper signal. A booklet titled *Engineer's Mini-Notebook 555 Timer IC Circuits* and the 555 chip can be purchased at Radio Shack for a combined price of less than $10. Use the "basic astable circuit" shown on page 7 of the booklet.

The output signal required is a 25-34 (30 optimum) Hz square wave, 20-80% (50% optimum) duty cycle, oscillating between 0 and 5 volts. The five volt reference voltage from the ECM should be used to supply power to the signal generator, the output wire goes to the ECM VATS wire, and a ground wire connects to the ECM ground. If you cannot build one yourself, a television repair shop can usually build one for you (check your local Yellow Pages).

If you are a car thief and want to use a 30 Hz signal generator to steal a VATS equipped Camaro or Corvette, the unit will not help you because the factory VATS *system* also includes a starter interlock so that the engine cannot be cranked. The signal generator only sends the proper signal to the ECM and will not defeat the factory starter interlock.

1992 & newer Corvettes use a much more sophisticated VATS signal that is incorporated into the Central Control Module (CCM) *and* the ECM, but the key resistances are the same as the earlier versions. Your best bet for this unit would be to purchase and aftermarket PROM with the VATS removed.

AIR CLEANERS & DUCTING

1985 S-10 Blazer with 1986 Corvette TPI and 700-R4 transmission.

The owner installed this engine without thinking in advance about the air cleaner ducting, or installing the MAF sensor.

Air cleaner ducting, and installing the MAF sensor are probably the biggest problem areas for most people who attempt a TPI conversion.

Due to the upper radiator hose routing, and the air conditioner hose routing, it is virtually impossible to install ducting for a remote air cleaner.

Note: The owner of this vehicle did not use JTR's *Chevrolet S-10 Truck V8 Conversion Manual.*

AIR CLEANERS & DUCTING

1985-1989 Tuned Port Injected engines use a MAF sensor to measure air flow into the engine. Some sort of air cleaner ducting is required from the MAF sensor to the throttle body. Because the MAF sensor is the primary means of measuring air flow into the engine, the ducting between the MAF sensor and the throttle body must not have leaks, or the engine will not run correctly.

A lot of people are under the impression that the MAF sensor causes a great restriction for the engine to breathe properly. The MAF is not noticeably restrictive on stock, or even moderately modified engines. As an example to how small the air cleaner ducting can get, the 1988-1992 Ford Mustangs with the 225 horsepower 5.0 liter V8 use a MAF sensor with a 2-1/8" orifice. That's right, a 2-1/8" diameter MAF sensor is sufficient for a 225 horsepower V8 engine. According to some GM engineers, the stock GM MAF sensor (which is considerably larger than the Ford unit) is good for over 350 horsepower.

The TPI MAF sensor's ends are 3-1/8" o.d. 3" i.d. rubber radiator hose (available at Truck supply stores) can be stretched over the ends. Gates® offers 3-1/8" i.d. rubber hose (part # 24250, green stripe) that fits perfectly over the MAF sensor. Many auto parts stores carry Gates® products.

The throttle body on a TPI engine is an oval shape with an outside circumference equivalent to a 4" i.d. rubber hose (also available at Truck supply stores).

The MAF sensor uses a "hot wire" which is somewhat susceptible to damage if the MAF sensor is mounted directly to the engine, or a vibrating body panel. Think of the "hot wire" as a light-bulb filament which can break if shaken or bumped. On Jaguars, and other smooth riding cars, we often mount the MAF sensor directly to the vehicle with a simple metal bracket. On _most_ vehicles, we rubber mount the MAF sensor to absorb vibrations and jolts.

Although the MAF sensors are considered by many to be fragile and unreliable, we have not had any problems with them in our own vehicles. However, we have seen MAF sensors damaged by water getting into the air cleaner, and then passing through the MAF sensor. If your "check engine" light comes on and the code is for the MAF sensor, don't automatically replace the MAF sensor. First, see if there is a factory bulletin for a MAF code for your engine. There are PROM updates for some of the early TPI engines. Go to your Chevrolet dealership for this information.

Second, check the ground wires on the back of the engine to make sure they are tight. If that doesn't solve the problem, replace the MAF relay and the MAF burn-off relay because most of the time the relays have failed, not the MAF sensor. Besides, relays are much cheaper than MAF sensors. The MAF sensors on the V8 TPI engines are actually very reliable, but the MAFs used on the early (1985-1988) 2.8 V6 front-wheel-drive cars had some reliability problems. A factory bulletin was issued for the front-wheel-drive 2.8 V6 MAF sensor that converted the MAF system to a speed-density system). Because of the MAF problems on the 2.8 V6, many people believe all MAF sensors are unreliable.

Chevrolet will be going back to the MAF system in 1994 because it is more accurate at measuring airflow than the speed-density system, and offers improved emissions control.

If a remote air cleaner and a MAF sensor will not fit into your engine compartment, you will need to install a 1990 or newer TPI engine, or convert your 1985-1989 TPI engine to the 1990 and newer speed-density system. A lot of people simply remove the MAF sensor and run an open-element air cleaner connected directly to the throttle body. The 1985-1989 engines will run quite well without the MAF sensor, but the "check engine" light will be turned on, and the engine will not run as well as it should. A lot of people are running 1985-1989 TPI engines this way, which has misled a lot of other people into believing that converting to the speed-density system is quite common.

CHANGING A MAF SENSOR SYSTEM TO A SPEED-DENSITY SYSTEM

If you have a complete 1985-1989 TPI engine, which operates with a MAF sensor, and want to make it a speed-density system in order to eliminate the MAF sensor, the remote air cleaner and ducting: it can be done, but it will probably be cheaper to purchase a 1990 wrecking yard engine and sell your 1985–1989 TPI engine.

Converting to a speed-density system will require (at the very minimum) the following:

1. Wiring harness from a 1990 or newer TPI engine. $ ~300 *
2. ECM from a 1990 or newer engine. $ ~240 **
3. PROM (computer chip) $ ~ 40
4. Knock sensor $ ~ 40
5. MAP sensor (part #16137039) $ ~ 50
6. Fuel pump relay $ ~ 15
7. Throttle position sensor $ ~ 55

The retail cost of a MAF sensor is:

1985	$ ~500
1986–1989	$ ~460
1988–1989	$ ~370

If you have a 1985-1989 engine that has a damaged MAF sensor, or you just don't have room for a MAF and the associated ducting, the cost may be justified. However, if you have not yet purchased an engine and don't want to install a MAF sensor, it will probably be a better deal to get a 1990 or newer engine.

Advantages of the "speed-density" (non-MAF sensor) TPI engine when compared to the MAF sensor equipped TPI engine.

1. No MAF sensor and wiring—can eliminate remote air cleaner and ducting.
2. No MAF relay and burn-off relay, and associated wiring.
3. No external Electronic Spark Control (ESC) module and wiring.

Disadvantages of 1990 or newer engines:

1. Not as adaptable to engine modifications with stock PROM.

* The 1989 and Older Camaro and Corvette ECMs use two multi-wire connectors. The 1990-1992 Camaro ECM uses three multi-wire connectors. The 1990-1991 Corvette ECM uses four multi-wire connectors. In other words, it is not a simple matter to adapt a pre-1990 wiring harness to a 1990 or newer ECM, but it can be done.

** 1990–1992 Camaro TPI ECM costs $110 plus exchange, the core charge is about $120. (The 1990–1992 V6 Camaro uses the same ECM, which is commonly found at wrecking yards.)

1990–1991 Corvette ECM costs $110 plus exchange, the core charge is about $150.

AIR CLEANERS

The most commonly used air cleaners for the TPI engine swaps are the canister styles used on Firebird TPI engines and the 1990 and newer V6 Camaros.

On the left is a Firebird air cleaner used on 1985-1987 V8 and V6 Firebirds. We call this a "side loader" air cleaner because the air cleaner ducting mounts to the side of the canister. The plastic cover on top of the air cleaner can be removed, as shown on the next page.

Second from the left is a "top loader" air cleaner used on V6 Camaros and Firebirds. The small inlet snout is used only on the V6 applications. If the snout is not removed on V8 applications, the restriction can actually cause the rubber ducting to the air cleaner to collapse, severely limiting power.

Third from the left is a V8 "top loader" air cleaner. Notice the size of the intake snout, compared to the V6 snout. This is a 1988 air cleaner because it uses 3 latches to hold the lid, instead of a long bolt which runs through the center of the air cleaner.

On the right are two air cleaner elements. Notice the size of the canister style element used in the Camaro/Firebird air cleaner as compared to a short "street rod" open element air cleaner. The "street rod" air cleaner cannot be used with a stock thermostat housing, and will not clear some of the accessories used on Corvette TPI engines.

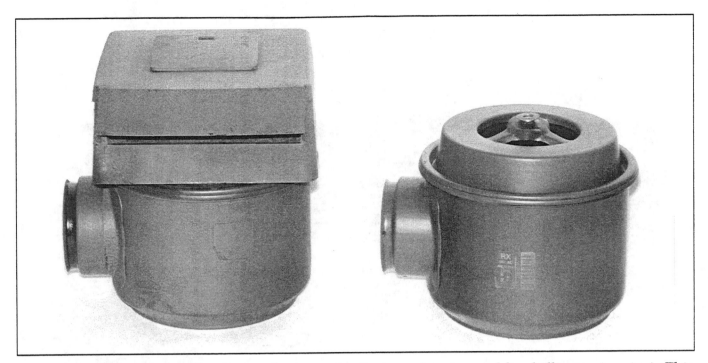

The "side loader" air cleaner has a plastic cover that can be removed by drilling out a rivet. This will make the filter a lot less bulky, and improve mounting possibilities.

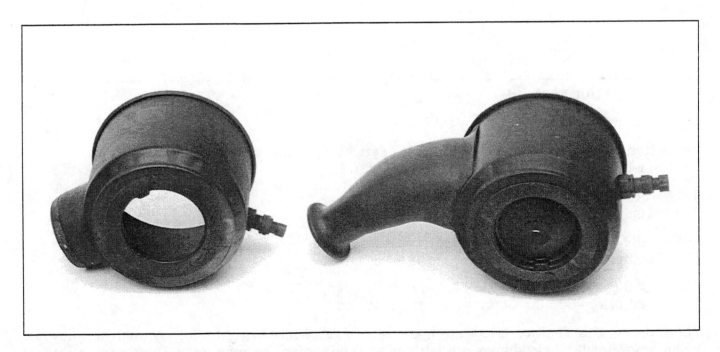

Some air cleaners don't have enclosed bottoms, and will require mods to fasten the lid if the Camaro/Firebird base plate is not used.

V6 air cleaners (shown above) use a temperature sending unit, which is what is sticking out of the right side of the above air cleaners. V8 air cleaners do not use temperature senders.

FACTORY GM DUCTING

From left to right:

1985-1989 Camaro and 1990-1992 Firebird Part #14094720
    List price ~$6.00, Connects to MAF, 3.12" i.d.

1985-1987 Firebird Part #10037612
    List price ~$73.00. Connects to ducting, 3.50" i.d.

1985-1989 Corvette part #14081891
    List price ~$7.00. Connects to MAF 3.12" i.d.

1988-1989 Firebird part #10055895
    List price ~$26.00. Connects to MAF 3.12" i.d.

The Camaro and Firebird ducts are made of rubber. While being flexible enough to allow for engine movement, their shapes are fairly rigid, and cannot be reshaped. The Corvette duct is made of thermoplastic, which allows it to be reshaped when properly heated (see next page).

CORVETTE DUCT

The top center duct is a stock Corvette duct (GM part#14081891). The other three Corvette ducts were modified by restraining the ducts to the desired shape and then putting them in a 350°F oven for 5 minutes.

The ends were fastened to metal that had enough thermal inertia to keep the ends cool enough to prevent the ends from deforming while in the oven.

Careful use of a heat gun, after installation will relieve any stress, and allow the ducting to conform exactly to the installation, without any stress on the intake components.

If you are going to modify the Corvette duct, they are inexpensive enough that you should buy several because it is easy to destroy the duct with improper heat application.

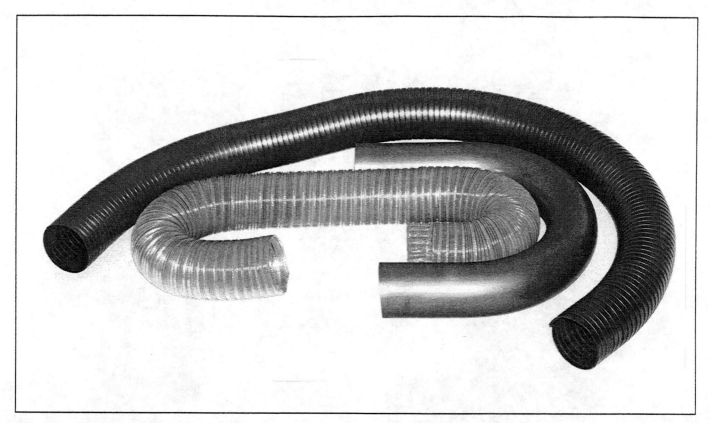

METAL AIR CLEANER DUCTING

The darkest tubing is 3" i.d. stainless steel flexible exhaust tubing. It does not hold its shape and does not make tight bends (minimum overall bend diameter is 25").

The U-bend is mandrel bent 3" o.d. exhaust tubing from a header manufacturer. The overall bend diameter is 15". It can be cut and welded to make differently shaped intake ducting.

The lightest colored ducting is 3" Z-flex tubing available for fireplace and wood stoves. It is made of stainless steel, and can easily be bent to conform to almost any air cleaner ducting requirements. The o.d. is 3-1/8" and the minimum overall bend diameter is 10". To purchase the stainless steel Z-Flex, look in the Yellow Pages under "Fireplaces." It costs about $10/foot.

Not shown. 3" aluminum dryer ducting. Available in most hardware stores, the aluminum drier ducting is too fragile for use in most automotive applications, but it is inexpensive enough to use for modeling purposes. It looks the same as the stainless steel Z-Flex.

To join the Z-Flex to a rubber coupling or hose, run a bead of "oxygen sensor safe" silicone sealant around the end of the Z-Flex tubing, and smooth it into the valleys of the corrugation. Let it dry and cure *before* using a rubber hose clamp and hose clamps. This way, it will seal properly, and can be removed easily for service.

"Oxygen sensor safe" silicone sealant must be used. If the wrong silicone sealant is used, the fumes will enter the induction system and be passed through to the oxygen sensor when the engine is running. This will damage the oxygen sensor.

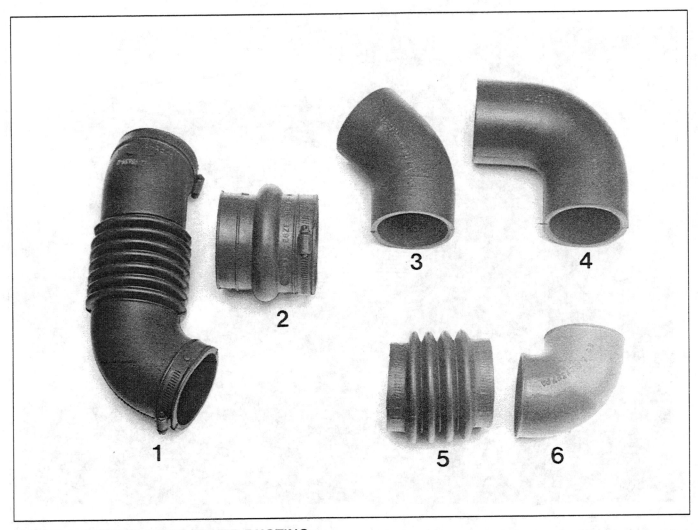

MISCELLANEOUS AIR CLEANER DUCTING

There are many different types of components that will help with air cleaner ducting for custom installations. We have used the following components for our swaps:

1. Duct from a 1992 Ford Mustang (part #9B659-D). 3" I.D., but stretchable to 3-1/8" I.D. Can be cut or sectioned for many types of installations.

2. Bellows from a 1992 Ford Mustang (part #9B647-AD). 3-1/2" I.D. Can be clamped over 3" I.D. components, and will fit over Stealth Conversions' nitrile rubber elbows.

3. Stealth Conversions' 45° nitrile rubber elbow. 3" I.D., 3.5" O.D., 3.6" centerline radius, I.D. will stretch to 3-1/8"

4. Stealth Conversions' 90° nitrile rubber elbow. 3" I.D., 3.5" O.D., 2.5" centerline radius, I.D. will stretch to 3-1/8".

5. Bellows from a 1978–1987 Jaguar XJ-6. 3-1/8" I.D., stretchable to 3-1/2" I.D.

6. 90° Aluminum Elbow from 1978–1987 Jaguar XJ-6. 3-1/8" O.D., 2-7/8" I.D.

For other air cleaner ducting, look at Datsuns, Volvos, front-wheel-drive GM cars, Fords, and whatever else you come across.

ODD, BUT IT WORKS!

There was no easy conventional way to mount the air cleaner and ducting for this 1941 Chevrolet Business Coupe. Also, there was very little room to install an engine driven cooling fan.

The owner decided that the air cleaner ducting could go up and backwards, and still fit under the stock hood. The components for the ducting are the Corvette thermoplastic duct attached to a Jaguar XJ-6 90° elbow.

Another advantage of this installation is that it leaves room for an engine-driven cooling fan.

Even though the owner preferred the installation on the previous page, this idea for routing the air cleaner ducting was mocked up and offers the advantage of being installed on cars with less hood clearance than the 1941 Chevrolet, and the air cleaner inlet can be more easily ducted for cooler, outside air.

Components used:

1. Corvette thermoplastic duct

2. Jaguar XJ-6 90° elbow (used on 1978-1986 XJ-6)

3. 3-1/8" i.d. flexible ducting from Buick Grand National (GM part #25525662, $30)

4. Stealth Conversions' 90° Nitrile elbow.

5. Side loader air cleaner.

COLD AIR DUCTING

It's a proven fact that cold air ducting can offer improved power compared to drawing heated air from the engine compartment.

The air cleaner on this Jaguar XJ-S was mounted so that it would receive cold air for more power. The 1990 Corvette radiator and the stock Jaguar air conditioning condenser were offset to the driver's side to allow the air cleaner snout (arrow) to receive cooler air than is available inside the engine compartment.

The foam above the air cleaner intake snout is to improve engine cooling by sealing the engine compartment so that cooling air goes through the radiator, not around it.

Components used:

1. Top loader air cleaner.
2. Two Stealth Conversions 90° Nitrile elbows
3. 1987 Firebird duct (part no. 10037612)
4. 3" o.d. metal tubing
5. 3" o.d. metal tubing for sleeves or liners
6. 3.5" i.d. rubber sleeve or Ford mustang bellows to attach Stealth elbow to top loader air cleaner.

BAFFLED

To prevent water from entering the air cleaner, a sheet metal baffle was fabricated and installed in front of the air cleaner snout. It is important to keep water out of the air cleaner. We have seen more than one MAF sensor damaged by water in the air cleaner.

Note on Cooling: Another advantage of the 1990 Corvette radiator in this installation is that its relatively thin core and side tanks allowed relocating the air conditioning condenser about 3/4" rearward from stock, which makes room for the Flex-a-lite model 10 electric cooling fan, which is mounted to the valence with a couple of simple brackets.

The TPI engine in this 1959 Jeep has accessories (power steering pump, alternator, and brackets) from a 1970–1976 Chevrolet Camaro/ Caprice/Malibu.

The ducting from the MAF sensor to the throttle-body makes a tight bend to the right and provides enough room for an engine-driven cooling fan, which (as mentioned in the chapter on cooling), will provide better cooling than an electric cooling fan.

The only criticism to this installation is that the MAF sensor is attached directly to the engine with a metal bracket. It should be rubber mounted so that engine vibrations don't damage the MAF sensor. In fact, it should be rubber mounted to the radiator support or to the fenders, and not to the engine.

The air cleaner is a "top loader" from a 1988–1992 Firebird, and the ducting from the air cleaner to the MAF sensor is from a 1988–1989 Firebird.

This type of air cleaner ducting can be used in many vehicles including full-size trucks and the G-bodies, which require engine-driven cooling fans when used for towing.

S-10 TRUCK WITH TPI

The air cleaner ducting can be routed many different ways. On this Chevrolet S-10 Blazer 4X4, a U-bend, based on a Paxton Supercharger duct, allows installing an engine-driven cooling fan. On 1987 and older Camaro/Firebird TPI engines, a similar U-bend or elbow can be used, but it will have to be installed on the passenger's side of the engine, and the battery may have to be relocated. (See TPI Volvo on page 1–10.)

The 90° fitting is often mistaken for conventional home plumbing parts, but it is from a 1978-1986 Jaguar XJ-6. The 90° fittings in the plumbing department of the hardware store will not fit this application.

The "bellows" allows normal engine movement without shaking the MAF sensor or damaging the other ducting. The bellows is also from a 1978-1986 Jaguar XJ-6. A Ford Mustang bellows could also be used.

The air cleaner is a "side loader" from a Pontiac Firebird, and is held to the inner fender with brackets made from steel strip.

The thermostat housing was also modified to reroute the upper radiator hose so that an engine-driven cooling fan could be used.

This air intake system offers the following advantages:

1. Engine driven cooling fan

2. MAF sensor mounted to the body, not to a vibrating engine.

3. Quiet. Very little intake noise

The disadvantages of this installation are a slight power loss at high rpm due to the restrictions caused by the bends, and the high cost of the parts (in excess of $300)

OPEN-ELEMENT AIR CLEANER

This open-element air cleaner (K&N part# RC-5000 or RC-5050) fits stock TPI engines with no modifications to the accessories. (K&N air cleaners are available at many auto parts stores.) If you are using a 1990 or newer TPI engine and have limited room for a remote air cleaner or need to run an engine-driven fan, this style of air cleaner can solve your problems.

Two compromises to this air cleaner are the fact that it receives hot air (which reduces power), and it is noisy. A remote air cleaner and ducting can be routed to receive outside air, and the ducting tends to muffle any intake noise.

This style of air cleaner is probably the most suitable for many engine swaps with limited room.

Note: Open-element air cleaners such as the K&N unit shown above are smog legal on 1990–1992 TPI engines because the TPI engines don't require a thermostatically controlled air cleaner and no other emissions components connect to the stock air cleaner assembly.

Also, open-element air cleaners are smog legal on the 1985–1989 TPI engine when used with the MAF sensor.

FUEL SYSTEM

Most people think that the wiring would be the most difficult part of installing the TPI/TBI engines into older vehicles. While the wiring may be the most difficult, the fuel system is the cause of the most "unsolvable" problems. There is a lot more to the fuel-injected fuel systems than many "experts" would know, so read this chapter carefully and you will know more than even some "experts."

FUEL-INJECTED FUEL TANKS

Camaros and Corvettes with fuel-injection have electric fuel pumps inside the fuel tanks. Externally, the fuel-injected tanks look the same as the carbureted fuel tanks, except there are three electrical wires attached to the sending unit on the injected tanks and two wires on the carbureted tanks. Some carbureted fuel tanks have fuel return lines; all fuel-injected tanks have fuel return lines. It is possible to install the in-tank electric fuel pump into some carbureted tanks, but the fuel-injected tanks have an internal baffle/reservoir that reduces fuel starvation during cornering, braking and acceleration when the fuel level is low.

On the Camaro, the baffle/reservoir looks like a simple trapezoid maze. It is about three inches high and made of a green plastic. It is fastened to the bottom of the tank with studs that are welded to the bottom of the tank. The baffle/reservoir cannot be retrofitted to non-fuel-injected tanks.

The baffle/reservoir works by maintaining the same fuel level as the rest of the tank during steady, level conditions. During cornering, or acceleration, the reservoir contains some of the fuel that would otherwise slosh to one side of the tank, away from the fuel pump. With fuel-injection, the engine will stall immediately if there is a loss of fuel pressure. Unlike a carburetor, which draws fuel into the engine by vacuum, fuel-injection uses pressure to spray fuel into the engine. If the fuel pressure drops, the fuel will not be sprayed into the engine, and it will immediatly stall. It is extremely important to have the correct fuel system when using fuel-injection.

If you can't get a fuel-injected tank for your application, or the cost of the fuel-injected tank is too expensive, you can use a remote fuel reservoir to prevent your vehicle from stalling when the fuel level is low. This is covered later in this chapter.

With fuel-injection, a fuel return line must be used to allow the fuel pressure regulator to bleed off excess fuel and control pressure. Also, the high pressure fuel pumps used with fuel-injected engines rely on fuel flowing through them to cool the electric motor. If the fuel flow is stopped or slowed, the electric motor will be damaged.

It is extremely important that a fuel return line is used, and that it goes into the main fuel tank. One "expert" recommends installing a tee into the fuel line going to the high pressure pump instead of installing a fuel return line all the way back to the main tank. The problem with doing that is the fuel gets heated as it goes through the fuel rail on the engine and if it is not returned to the tank, it will boil and cause vapor lock. This is why we wonder if these "experts" have actually driven vehicles that they claim to have worked on.

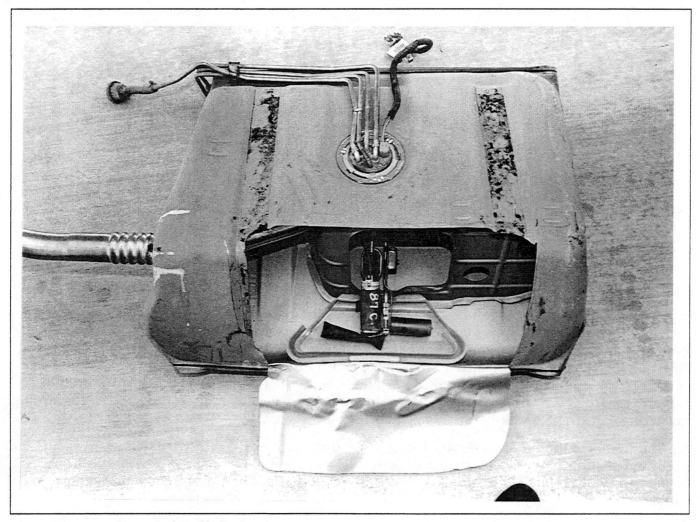

IT'S WHAT'S INSIDE THAT COUNTS

This is a fuel tank from a fuel-injected Camaro that has been cut open to show an example of the fuel pump and the "maze-like" baffle/reservoir. Although the reservoir is only about three inches deep in this application, it makes a huge difference when the fuel level is low. Without the reservoir, the fuel-injected engine will suffer from fuel starvation during moderate cornering, acceleration, or braking, even with 1/4 tank of fuel. If the intank pump sucks air on a regular basis, pump life will be reduced.

If you are installing a fuel-injected engine into a vehicle that was originally carbureted, but was available with fuel-injection in later model years, you may be able to install the complete fuel-injected tank into your vehicle.

The valve on the top left of the photo is a pressure relief valve. It is used to vent fuel vapors to the atmosphere if vapors build up too quickly for the evaporative emissions controls. Because the fuel returned to the tank is heated from the fuel rails on the engine, vapor build-up can be a problem with the fuel-injected engines, unless properly vented.

IN-TANK PUMP ASSEMBLY

This is the in-tank fuel pump/fuel level sending unit assembly for a 1990 TPI Camaro. The assembly installs through the top of the tank. The factory in-tank fuel pumps are very reliable and quiet, but they can fail if run dry for more than a few seconds.

The pump has a strainer at the pick-up to prevent large foreign objects from damaging the pump. The strainer also acts as a "wick" to catch all of the fuel available.

The electric fuel pump will not cause the fuel tank to explode because fuel has to be mixed with the proper ratio of oxygen (air) to burn. The fuel/air ratio inside the tank is too rich to support combustion if a spark were to occur. Fuel is non-conductive, so bare electrical wires are not a problem as long as they don't contact anything that is electrically conducting.

Notice that the fuel return line extends all

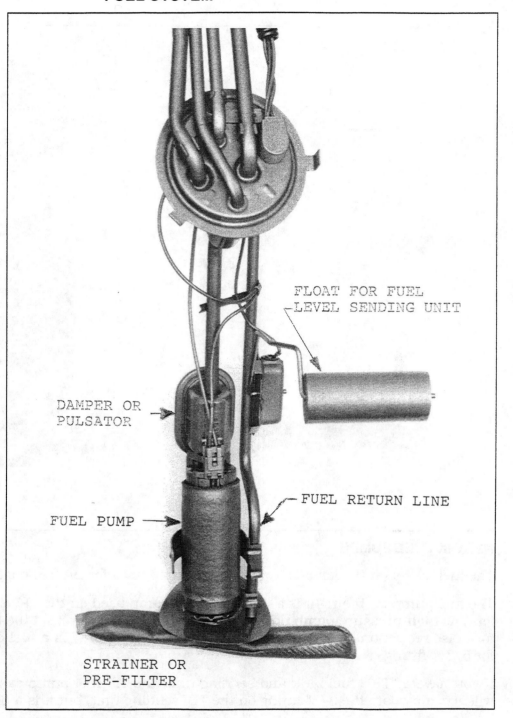

FLOAT FOR FUEL LEVEL SENDING UNIT

DAMPER OR PULSATOR

FUEL RETURN LINE

FUEL PUMP

STRAINER OR PRE-FILTER

the way to the bottom of the tank. This is for two reasons.

1. To prevent fuel aeration.
2. To return fuel into the fuel baffle/reservoir.

The damper or pulsator is only used on the TPI engines and not on the TBI engines. Its purpose is to quiet or dampen the fuel pulsations caused by the injectors opening and closing, and to smooth or steady the flow of fuel.

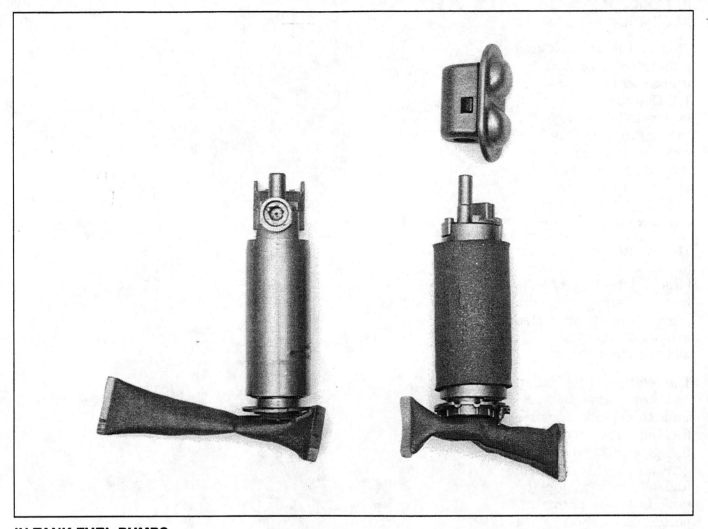

IN-TANK FUEL PUMPS

The fuel pump on the left is a low pressure pump used for the TBI engines. The outlet is 3/8".

The fuel pump on the right is a high pressure pump used on the TPI engines. It has a 5/16" outlet. The high-pressure pump normally has a rubber sleeve around the body of the pump which is for noise reduction. The part above the high-pressure pump is a fuel damper, which is designed for 5/16" fittings.

If you have a "TBI" fuel tank and sending unit, the TPI fuel pump can be installed. The damper will accommodate the 3/8" fitting on the TBI sending unit, but it is a tight squeeze.

There is a lot more to fuel pumps than meets the eye. For example, the above fuel pumps have check valves to prevent fuel from flowing backwards into the tank when the engine is turned off.

The factory in-tank pumps are quite reliable; however, they will fail if run dry. The pump life will be reduced if the fuel filter gets clogged, so it is a good idea to change fuel filters at 10,000 mile intervals.

According to a large number of Chevrolet mechanics, about half of the "no start" complaints on the fuel-injected engines are for failed fuel pumps. It's not that the pumps are unreliable, it's because the fuel-injected engines are so good that the most common reason for them not starting is a failed fuel pump. That's not to say the fuel-injected engines are not brought in for drivability problems (rough idle, check engine light, etc.). It's just that they are rarely brought in for not running.

FUEL SYSTEM

EXTERNAL FUEL PUMP SYSTEMS

An "external fuel pump system" will normally be required for vehicles that were not available with fuel-injection or in-tank pumps. An "external fuel pump system" consists of

1. An external reservoir to prevent stalling caused by fuel starvation

2. An external low-pressure fuel pump to feed the external reservoir

3. An external high-pressure fuel pump to feed the engine

4. The appropriate fuel lines, fittings, and filters.

An "external fuel pump system" is more complicated than a fuel-injected in-tank pump system, but for roadside serviceability, the external fuel pumps are a lot easier to change than in-tank pumps. Replacing an in-tank pump can take over 4 hours on some vehicles.

An external fuel reservoir is, quite simply, a small fuel tank that is installed on fuel-injection installations to prevent stalling caused by fuel starvation during abrupt maneuvers when the fuel tank is less than 1/4 full. The external reservoir does not need to hold much fuel. 1/2 cup (4 ounces) is enough fuel for most engines to run around clover leaf freeway on-ramps. In a sense, the external reservoir acts like the float bowl on a carburetor. It does not need to hold a lot of fuel, it just needs to supply fuel during abrupt maneuvers when the fuel pick-up tube in the main tank is sucking air.

You can build your own remote fuel reservoir, but you had better have some good fabricating skills because fuel leaks not only smell bad, they can be dangerous.

A remote reservoir requires four fittings:

1. One to supply the reservoir with fuel

2. One to supply the high pressure pump

3. One for the return from the engine

4. One for a return to the main tank, to expel any air in the remote reservoir.

The fitting going to the high-pressure fuel pump must be mounted at the bottom of the remote reservoir so that it always receives fuel. The return line going to the main tank must be mounted at the top of the reservoir to expel air. The supply line coming from the main tank should be mounted high so that the fuel does not drain backwards into the main tank when the engine is turned off. The fuel line returning from the engine can be installed anywhere on the remote reservoir.

IF YOU DO NOT HAVE FOUR FUEL LINES GOING TO THE REMOTE RESERVOIR, IT WILL NOT WORK!

REMOTE FUEL RESERVOIR

The above reservoir is a home built unit. It holds about 12 ounces of fuel. Note that the reservoir has five 1/4" NPT female fittings, yet only four are required for an external reservoir. The "extra" fitting allows positioning the reservoir vertically or horizontally to best suit the space available in the vehicle.

It is important not to pressurize the remote reservoir because the pressure will feed back to the fuel pressure regulator on the engine, causing increased fuel pressure at the engine. When the fuel lines are properly connected to the fuel reservoir, there will be very little pressure (less than 2 pis) inside the reservoir. The only place that the fuel will be under high pressure is between the high pressure fuel pump and the engine.

Another benefit of the remote reservoir is that it reduces vapor build-up in the fuel tank by recirculating some of the fuel warmed by the engine. The warmed fuel will provide little difference in engine performance (see the pressure releif valve shown on page 10–2).

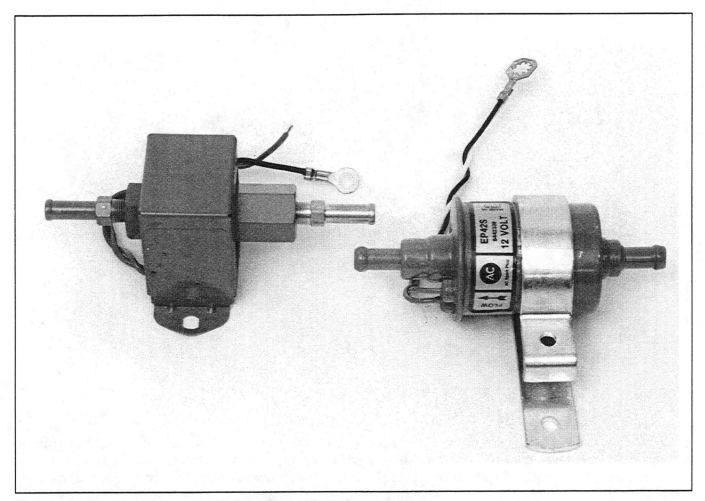

LOW-PRESSURE FUEL PUMPS TO FEED THE RESERVOIR

Some low-pressure fuel pumps are not suitable for use with fuel return lines because the pump must run continuously. Bellows type pumps are not normally suitable for supplying fuel to the remote sump because they will wear out prematurely.

The above pumps are solenoid pumps. They are designed to work with fuel return lines and can run continuously.

The pump on the left is used in some older Mazda cars and trucks as original equipment. It is a very reliable pump and is fairly inexpensive (about $40) and is readily available at most auto parts stores. It is sold under various names: Faucet, TRW, and Purolator, to name a few. Several models are made, with flow ratings of 20 gallons/hour at 2 psi to 30 gallons/hour at 5 psi. At 1/2 psi (about normal for the remote reservoir), the above pump (which is rated at 20 gallons/hour at 2 psi) flows over 30 gallons per hour—more than enough to supply a remote reservoir for a 454 cubic inch big block. The above pump draws less than 1 amp of current at 12 volts. It has 1/8" npt (national pipe threads) inlet and outlet fittings.

The pump on the right is an AC-Delco solenoid pump, model EP42S. It is very reliable and is available at any Chevrolet dealer. It has 3/8" inlet and outlet fittings.

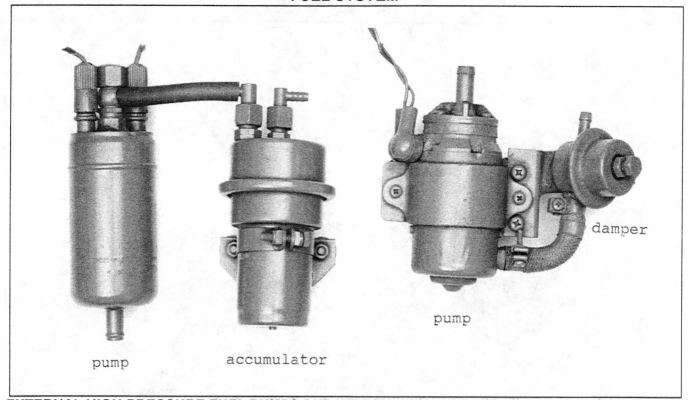

pump   accumulator   pump   damper

EXTERNAL HIGH PRESSURE FUEL PUMPS AND WRECKING YARD FUEL PUMPS

Many vehicles in the wrecking yards have externally mounted high pressure fuel pumps that will adequately supply a 350 TPI engine. At the local "Pick Your Part," we can purchase these pumps for about $25. Remember, according to the Chevrolet mechanics we know, about 1/2 of the "no-start" problems are caused by bad fuel pumps. It is usually a good idea to buy a new pump.

The pump on the left is a Bosch pump and accumulator (similar to a damper) from an Audi that suffered from "unintended DEceleration." The pump is rated at 30 gallons/hour at 60 psi. The inlet is 1/2". The outlet is only 1/4", but 1/4" to 5/16" or 3/8" hose adapters can easily be made using brass fittings available at hardware stores and auto parts stores.

The pump and damper on the right is from a Datsun 200 SX. The inlet is 1/2" and the outlet is 5/16". This pump is rated at 22 gallons/hour at 43 psi, which is adequate for a stock 305 TPI. The rubber isolated mounting bracket is easily mounted to most vehicles. A high pressure pump from a 280Z appears to flow more than the 200 SX pump and is adequate for 350 TPI engines.

At the wrecking yard, Datsun 280Zs and ZXs, Volvo 240 and 260 models, Volkswagen Rabbits and Jettas, and some Audis are your best source for external high pressure fuel pumps. Many of the older BMWs also use external high pressure fuel pumps.

Most of the newer fuel-injected cars and trucks (both import and domestic) use in-tank pumps.

You can use the above fuel pumps for the TBI engines because the pressure regulator on the engine will bypass the fuel. The only problem we have seen is that the pump will run at a higher speed because of the lower pressure, and may wear out prematurely. We have successfully installed large (25 watt) 1-2 ohm power resistors in the power wire going to the fuel pump to slow it down so that the pump sounds like it's running at a normal speed. The resistor will get warm (or even hot) so it is important to mount the resistor where it can dissipate heat. Power resistors are available at most electronics stores. To find one near you, look in the Yellow Pages under "Electronics Parts and Supplies." Ballast resistors for the ignition system can also be used, although it may be necessary to install two ballast resistors in parallel for the desired results.

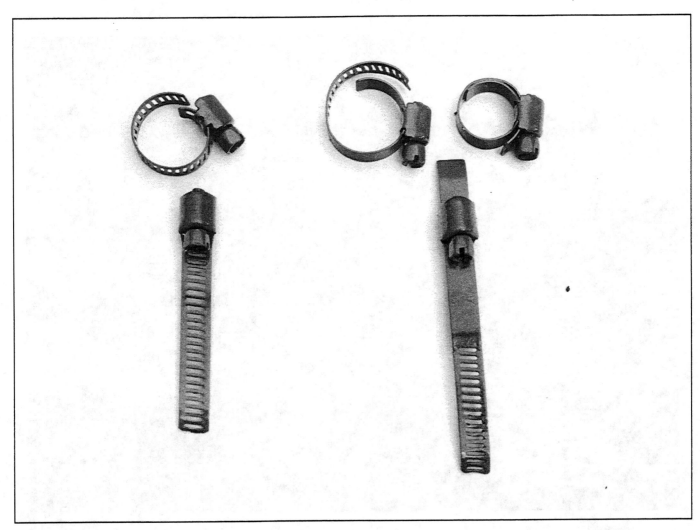

HOSE CLAMPS

On the left are conventional hose clamps.

On the right are fuel-injection hose clamps which are designed for higher pressure than conventional hose clamps. Notice how the fuel-injection hose clamps have a section of unslotted clamp and a liner that protects the hose from being cut by the slots in the clamp to protect the hose under the higher pressures used with fuel-injection.

The 1985 and newer Corvettes and Camaros use fuel-injection hose clamps at the fuel tank fittings. At the engine, metric o-ring fittings are used for the fuel hose connections, but the fuel hoses can be cut, and fuel-injection hose clamps can be used to secure the hoses to conventional hose fittings. Many foreign cars use hose clamps.

CUSTOM FUEL LINES

The rubber fuel lines connecting to the fuel rail were custom made for this application at a hydraulic hose store. If you need something special for your vehicle, look in the yellow pages under "Hydraulic Equipment and Supplies." These businesses can make custom hoses for fuel lines, power steering hoses, air conditioning hoses, etc.

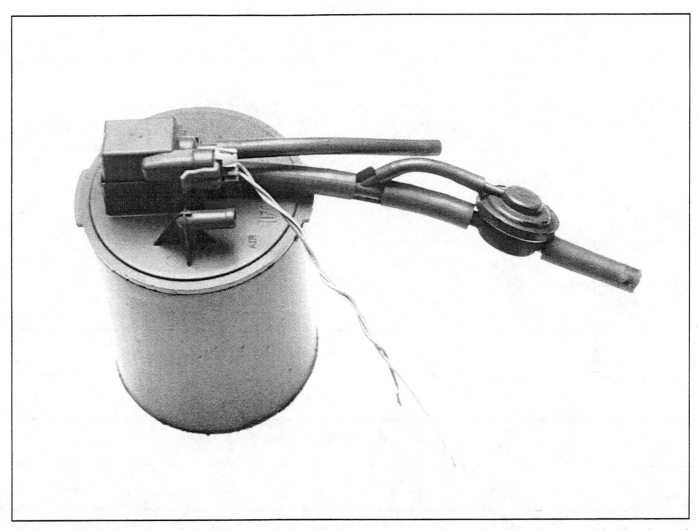

This is the charcoal canister from a 1990 TPI Camaro. It uses an electrically-controlled solenoid valve to control canister purging. The canister will not purge unless the vehicle speed sensor is installed. TBI trucks do not use an electrically-controlled purge valve.

If you are having difficulties with your charcoal canister hose routing, look at a vehicle that has the same engine that you are using. The 1990 TPI Camaro uses only one valve for the charcoal canister, but 1989 and older TPI engines use two valves. If the valves are hooked up to the wrong hoses, or the valve is not correct for the application, the tank pressure can get extremely high, or engine vacuum can collapse the tank. Typical results of a charcoal canister that is not hooked up properly are excessive fuel tank pressure, gas fumes, poor drivability, collapsed fuel tanks, and leaks.

Note: It is normal to hear a slight "whoosh" when removing the gas cap on a fuel tank that is fitted with evaporative emission controls because the valves try to seal the gas vapors in the tank. But if you hear the fuel tank collapsing on itself, or if you smell fumes, something is definitely wrong and needs to be fixed.

FUEL SYSTEM
Note Page

EXHAUST

HEADERS AND KNOCK SENSOR

The "street rod" headers on this 1988 305 TPI engine in a 1941 Chevrolet interfered with the knock sensor. The boss on the drivers side of the engine (normally used for a mechanical clutch linkage) was re-threaded with a 1/4 n.p.t. tap. The knock sensor (arrow) was then screwed into the boss. The wiring was rerouted and the knock sensor works fine.

The owner removed the AIR pump from this engine to "clean-up" the looks of the engine compartment. Removing the AIR pump and the wiring on the 1985-1992 engines will not affect the ECM, or engine operation.

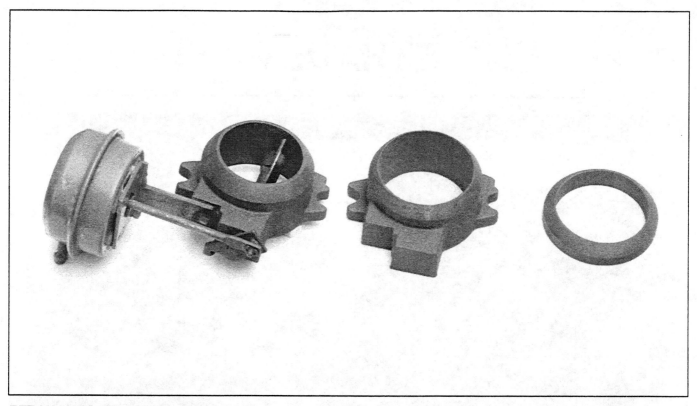

EFE VALVES, SPACERS AND SEALS

On the left is an EFE valve (Early Fuel Evaporation) used on most 1975–1987 *carbureted* Chevrolet V8s. During warm-up, it is used to block the exhaust gases and force them through the exhaust crossover passage in the intake manifold to improve fuel vaporization and distribution during warm-up.

The 1985–1989 *fuel-injected* Camaros use a spacer (center) which is basically an EFE valve without the valve. The spacer is used because it allows the same headpipes on both carbureted and fuel-injected engines.

The part on the right is called a "seal." It is used on 1990–1992 V8 Camaros on the passenger's side exhaust manifold outlet.

EFE valves, spacers and seals come in different sizes, so make sure you install the correct part for your application. In tight installations, our muffler shop will install the shorter seal (and studs) to improve clearance.

HEAT SHIELDS

The exhaust system on your engine swap can cause a lot of heat related problems.

The simple heat shield shown above is welded to the exhaust pipe and is an excellent solution for protecting the steering rack boot from heat damage on this Jaguar XJ-6.

The heat shield is a piece of 18-gauge sheet metal, about 2" wide, and about 6" long. This type of heat shield can be installed to protect starters, brake lines, wiring, suspension bushings, etc.

Thermo-Tec® heat insulation is an excellent product for protecting parts from heat. This product is available at many automotive parts stores and speed shops.

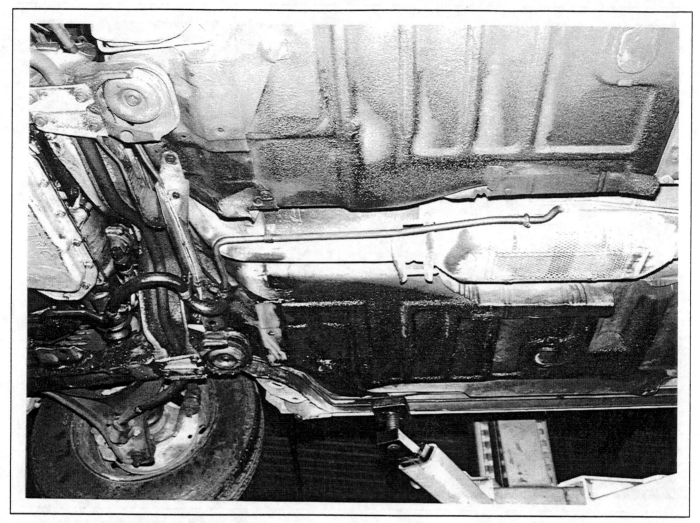

AIR TUBE TO CATALYTIC CONVERTER

The AIR tube for the catalytic converter can be easily attached to the air pump with a rubber hose connected to the metal tube. The hose is specially designed for this application and most muffler shops carry the tubing.

The metal tube should extend far enough from the catalytic converter and exhaust so that the rubber hose does not get burned. The metal tube can be secured to the exhaust pipe with radiator hose clamps.

The above photo shows a stock, 1982 front-wheel-drive Buick Century with a 3.0 V6.

If you are running dual catalytic converters, a tee can be made to supply air to both converters.

DUAL CATALYTIC CONVERTERS AND DUAL EXHAUST

The installation of dual catalytic converters on some engine swaps is a gray area. The Bureau of Automotive Repair (BAR), which controls the Referee Stations in California, has not, at the time of this printing, put in writing, the rules on installing dual catalytic converters for engine changes. However, the Referee Station will allow dual catalytic converters on an individual basis, but you should first verify that they will allow dual "cats" for your particular vehicle and engine **before** you have dual cats installed.

The Referee Stations tend to use the following rules for catalytic converters with engine swaps:

1. They will not allow dual cats if the vehicle and engine did not offer dual cats.

2. Cars or trucks that did not come with any catalytic converters are not required to run a catalytic converter with a cat-type of engine because the chassis was not designed for a catalytic converter and without proper heat shields and other protective measures, the catalytic converter and the exhaust system behind the catalytic converter may be a fire hazard.

   Exception: Diesel powered vehicles that were offered with gasoline engines and catalytic converters will require cats.

3. Because cars and trucks that did not come with any catalytic converters are not required to have catalytic converters, they are allowed to run dual catalytic converters even if the engine installed did not run dual cats.

   Exception: Diesel powered vehicles that were offered with gasoline engines and catalytic converters will require cats.

4. If the chassis was equipped with dual catalytic converters (such as the V-12 Jaguars) and the engine was not offered with dual catalytic converters, the referee station will allow dual catalytic converters.

5. If the engine was offered with dual catalytic converters and the chassis only came with a single converter, the referee station may allow dual catalytic converters if they are no further away from the engine than when the engine was in its original application. The location of the converters is very important because the closer they are to the engine, the quicker they will "light-off" and reduce pollutants.

6. If the vehicle originally had a two-way converter, and the engine installed came with a three-way converter, the vehicle will be required to have a three-way converter.

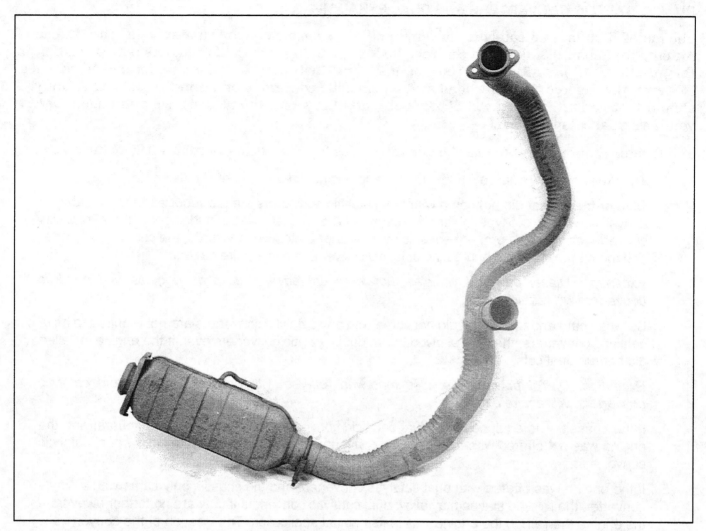

This is the factory headpipe and catalytic converter that is used on many 1986-1992 TPI-equipped Firebirds and Camaros. The headpipes are 2-1/2" double wall (.095" wall thickness) joining into a 2-3/4" tube that runs to the 3" inlet catalytic converter.

305 TBI Camaros and Firebirds, and some 1990-1992 305 TPI Camaros and Firebirds use a similar configuration, but with 2" headpipes joining into a 2-1/2" tube that connects to a 2-1/2" inlet catalytic converter.

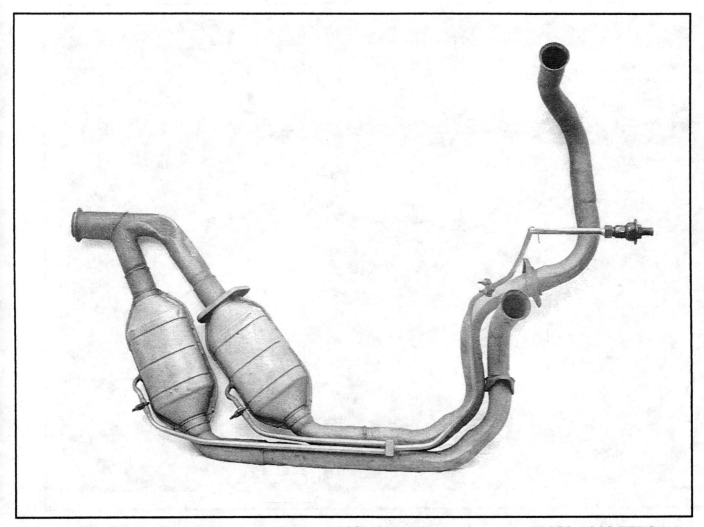

This is a factory dual catalytic converter assembly that was used on some 1989-1992 TPI Camaros and Firebirds (option code N10). This part retails for about $975.

The significance of this dual catalytic converter option is that it sets precedence to allow true dual exhaust on vehicles that are using the 1989-1992 Camaro/Firebird TPI engines (not Corvette). However, the catalytic converters must be placed close to the engine, and not way back where they will not get hot enough to be effective. The headpipe lengths on this catalytic converter assembly are about 50" for the passenger's side, and about 60" for the driver's side. The single wall headpipes are 2-1/4" o.d. and the wall thickness is about .062". The pipes after the converter are 2-1/2", and they join into a single 2-3/4" pipe. Because of the lack of double wall headpipes on this exhaust configuration, we believe that Chevrolet uses double wall headpipes for noise suppression, and not for quicker catalytic converter "light-off."

As for performance gains, Chevrolet rates the 1990-1992 manual transmission 305 TPI Camaro engine at 230 HP with dual Cats, and 205 hp with the single cat.

Also, the 1993 Corvette LT1 is rated at 300 HP and the 1993 Camaro LT1 is rated at 275 HP. The Corvette runs dual catalytic converters and the Camaro runs a single catalytic converter. The Corvette also has less restrictive air cleaner ducting and different exhaust manifolds, but we believe most of the performance difference is because of the exhaust system.

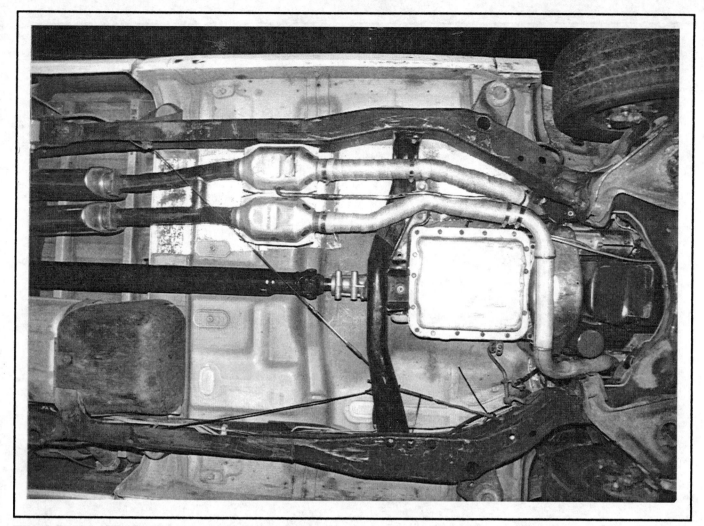

TRUE DUAL EXHAUST

This is a true dual exhaust on a 1987 GMC S-15 Truck[1]. Note the Thermo-Tec™ heat shielding and insulation installed above the exhaust system, and how the headpipes are wrapped to keep the heat of the exhaust from going into the cab. Dual catalytic converters produce lots of heat. Also note the crossover pipe behind the catalytic converters.

The A.I.R. tube to the catalytic converters is te'ed into both converters.

From what we have seen, installing dual catalytic converters on a vehicle with a 1989-1992 TPI engine will probably be allowed on an "individual basis" at the Referee Station. Again, this is a gray area, but we feel that showing what has been allowed will ease the allowance of dual catalytic converters on your vehicle if you are using a 1989-1992 Camaro/Firebird TPI engine, and the converters are located close to the engine.

1.Did you know that JTR has a *Chevrolet S-10 Truck V8 Conversion Manual* that also works for GMC S-15 Trucks? The truck shown above runs 103 mph in the quarter mile and is completely smog legal.

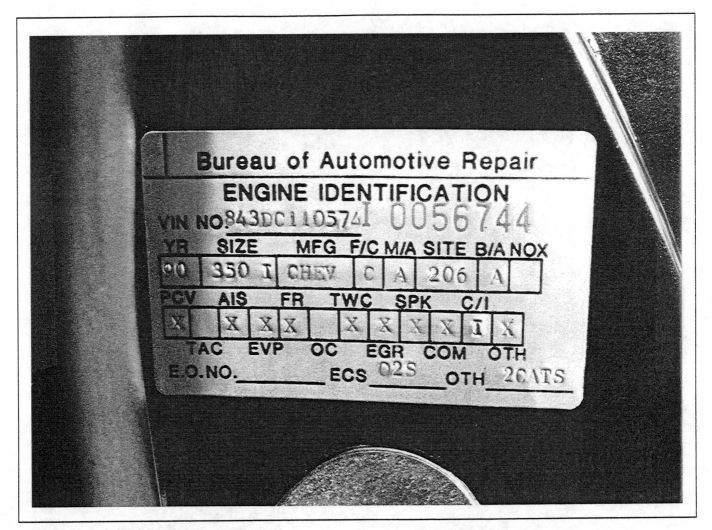

APPROVED WITH "2 CATS"

This is the engine identification tag used by the Bureau of Automotive Repair (BAR) for engine swaps. The car is a 1983 Jaguar XJ-S with a 1990 Corvette TPI engine.

Notice that "2CATS" listed on the tag in the lower right corner. This shows that the Referee station approved the dual catalytic converters. More importantly, it lets any smog inspector or muffler shop know that the dual exhaust is smog legal on this particular car.

FOUR CAT JAGUAR

1983 Jaguar XJ-S with 1990 Corvette engine. The Jaguar exhaust system is mostly stock, except for the short headpipes which connect the Jaguar exhaust system to the Chevrolet exhaust manifolds. This vehicle comes with four catalytic converters, two on each side. The front converters are the NO_x reducing converters, and the rear are oxidizing converters. As you can see, this is a tight fit, and the stock Jaguar heat shields are not yet installed.

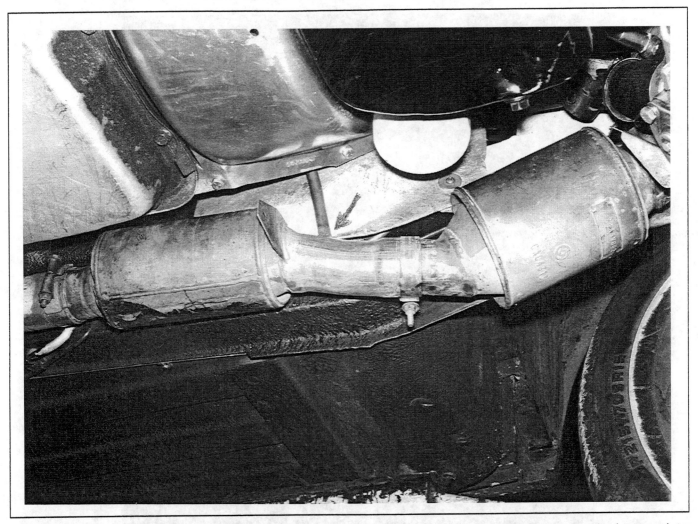

The AIR tube (arrow) was installed between the two catalytic converters to supply air (oxygen) to the oxidizing converter. This allows the proper smog hook-ups to the Chevrolet AIR pump. The Jaguar exhaust was not originally equipped with AIR tubes. Attaching the AIR tube is a somewhat gray area, but the Referee Station allowed it in this particular situation. Ford vehicles (Mustangs and Lincoln Mk 7) have a similar exhaust system (maybe that's why Ford bought Jaguar).

TYPICAL V8 JAGUAR

1981 Jaguar XJ-6 with 1987 350 TPI/700-R4 transmission. This is a more typical V8 Jaguar exhaust system, with a single catalytic converter mounted behind the transmission and a "Y" pipe joining the headpipes before the catalytic converter.

This is the only place to install a large, single catalytic converter on this chassis. 1982-1991 Corvettes use a similar exhaust system with the catalytic converter installed behind the transmission, but the 1986-1991 models use, in addition, two small "light-off" converters installed close to the exhaust manifolds, which are quite similar to the "light-off" converters used on Ford Mustangs.

At least one company has received EPA approval for a Mustang "high performance" replacement catalytic converter exhaust system that does not use the "light-off" converters, so this is part of the reasoning that the system pictured above is considered legal for this engine swap.

VEHICLE SPEED SENSOR

The biggest obstacle for most people who install the TPI/TBI engines into their vehicles is the VSS (Vehicle Speed Sensor). At the time of this writing, some of the aftermarket wiring harnesses don't use a VSS. They simply ground the P/N (Park/Neutral) wire so that the ECM always thinks the vehicle is in park. If they didn't ground the P/N wire, the "Check Engine" light would always be turned on. Because of the importance of the vehicle speed sensor, we cannot recommend these harnesses. If you have already purchased a harness which does not use a VSS, you can add the VSS and properly connect the P/N wire on automatic transmission vehicles, or remove it on cars with manual transmissions.

Basically, the VSS tells the ECM how fast the vehicle is going. Most people think the VSS is only used for the lock-up torque converter. The VSS is also used to control the EGR valve, the charcoal canister purge valve, the electric cooling fans, and the idle speed. This is all explained in the Chevrolet shop manual (available from Helm at (800)782-4356), which is required reading for installing the TPI/TBI engine into your vehicle.

It must be emphasized that the VSS is used to control the idle speed when the vehicle is moving. Without the VSS, a vehicle may have stalling problems under certain conditions. Needless to say, this could be very dangerous. The reason an engine not equipped with a VSS may stall is because when the ECM has the signals that indicate the engine should be idling (foot off the gas pedal, vehicle moving less than 2 m.p.h.), *idle speed* is *closed loop* (which is not the same as the O_2 sensor running closed loop) and the ECM will try to maintain a *programmed* idle speed. If the vehicle is moving, the ECM opens the IAC (idle air control) a programmed amount, regardless of engine speed, which is usually a position that will make the engine idle about 50-100 r.p.m. above the stationary *programmed* idle speed. Stalling can occur when the vehicle is in the over-run condition (foot off the gas pedal, engine speed above the programmed idle speed) because the ECM will try to lower the idle speed to the stationary programmed speed. The IAC may not be able to open rapidly enough to prevent the engine from stalling.

Raising the minimum idle speed with the adjusting screw can eliminate stalling, but the engine will still not run optimally without a VSS.

A lot of people think that running "closed loop" is best for fuel mileage. Closed loop simply means that the oxygen sensor is being used to monitor the fuel/air ratio. Some of the Chevrolet fuel-injected engines are programmed to run lean under certain conditions (called "highway mode") to improve fuel mileage during steady cruise conditions. Without a VSS, the ECM will not get the correct signals to run the engine for best fuel mileage. There are a lot of programs in the ECM which depend on the VSS. Without a VSS, your factory TPI/TBI engine will not run properly. For best operation, the Chevrolet fuel-injected engines require *all* sensors to be connected and functioning.

There are two types of VSS signals required by the ECM: The two-pulse square wave used on all TBI engines, all computer-controlled-carbureted engines, and on 1985-1989 TPI engines. A four-pulse sine-wave signal is required by the 1990-1992 TPI engines, and 1990-1992 Camaro 3.1 V6 engines.

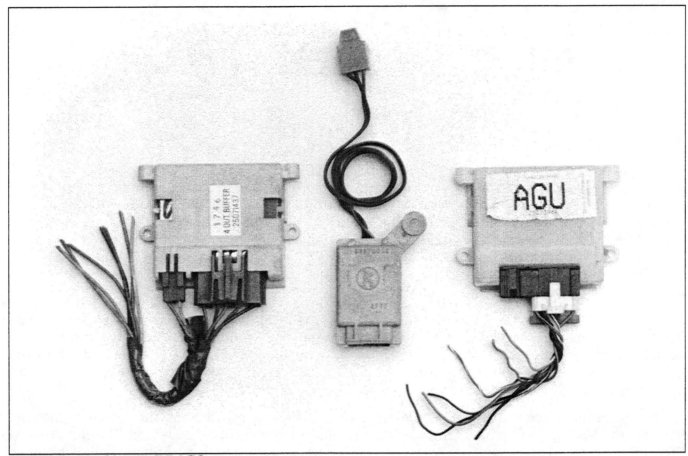

VSS, BUFFERS, AND DRACS

On the left is a "4-output vehicle speed buffer" used on vehicles with electric speedometers. It gets the vehicle speed signal from a 4-pulse sine-wave generator mounted at the transmission, and converts the sine-wave into a square wave signal for the ECM, speedometer, cruise control, and on some models, the radio (to control volume with vehicle speed). 1990 and newer TPI engines have the buffer incorporated into the ECM, and the ECM outputs the square wave to the speedometer, cruise control and radio.

In the center is a two-output vehicle speed buffer used on vehicles with cable driven speedometers. The piece on top is called the "optic head" and it mounts to the speedometer and senses vehicle speed through a light beam and reflector on the speedometer (it is more fully explained in the Camaro and Firebird shop manuals, available from Helm). The buffer (the lower part) converts the reflected light signal into a 2-pulse square wave signal for the ECM and cruise control. The two-output vehicle speed buffer is normally mounted under the dash on the driver's side, and held in place with a tie wrap.

On the right is a "DRAC" (Digital Ratio Adapter Controller) from a 1989-1992 S-10 truck, Astro Vans and 1990-1992 full-size trucks. Earlier (1987-1989) Full-size trucks use a programmable DRAC that is incorporated into the instrument panel. All Chevrolet trucks with rear wheel anti-lock brakes (1989 and newer) use electric speedometers. The rear wheel speed is monitored by a sensor mounted on the output shaft of the transmission, where a speedometer cable would normally be installed (see next page). The signal (40 pulses per driveshaft revolution) goes to the DRAC which divides and conditions the signal for the electric speedometer, ECM, cruise control and anti-lock brakes. There are different DRAC modules for different gear ratios and tire sizes.

The newer trucks with electronically controlled transmissions use a buffer that is similar to a DRAC in that it sends signals to the speedometer, anti-lock brakes, and cruise control, but the signal from the buffer sends out different signals than the DRAC.

TRUCK VEHICLE SPEED SENSORS

The part that looks like a gear (in the center) is a 40 tooth reluctor ring that is used on the trucks with electric speedometers.

On the left of the reluctor ring is the VSS used on trucks with the 700-R4 transmision.

On the far right is the VSS used on the S-10 Trucks with the Borg-Warner 5-speed transmissions. a slightly different unit is used on the trucks with the Mucie-Getrag or New Venture transmissions.

The Vehicle Speed Sensors supply an AC (alternating current) to the DRAC module or Buffer on trucks. The DRAC or Buffer then converts the signal for the speedometer, anti-lock brakes, cruise control, and engine.

If you are installing a TPI engine and transmission into your late-model truck, the VSS and reluctor ring must be installed onto the TPI transmission. If you have a 1990 or newer TPI engine, you will also need Stealth Conversions vehicle speed sensor module (part #4PT) to condition the signal for the 1990-1992 TPI ECM.

The reluctor ring is difficult to install without the proper equipment due to the interference fit of the reluctor ring onto the output shaft. However, we have increased the inside diameter of the reluctor ring by filing or sanding, and roughed up the transmission output shaft (for adhesive reasons), and glued the reluctor ring to the output shaft with a good quality epoxy.

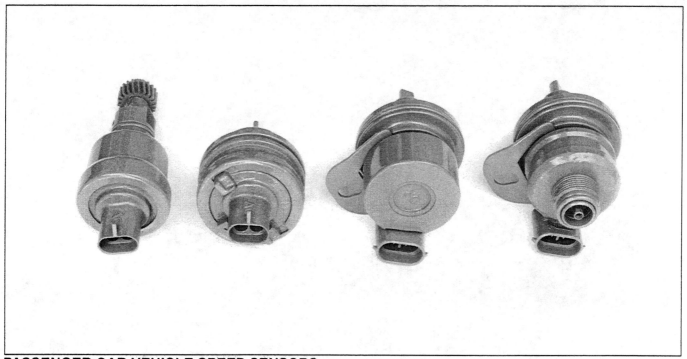

PASSENGER CAR VEHICLE SPEED SENSORS

On the left is the 4-pulse VSS used on manual transmission Camaros with electric speedometers.

Second from the left is the 4-pulse VSS used on 1984 and newer Corvettes.

Third from the left is the 4-pulse VSS used on Camaros with automatic transmissions and electric speedometers.

On the far right is the Stealth Coversions' 4-pulse integral VSS/speedometer sleeve. This VSS has provisions for using a standard speedometer cable. If you are installing a 1990-1992 TPI engine (or 1990-1992 Camaro V6) with a 700-R4 transmission or ZF six-speed into a vehicle with a mechanical speedometer, this unit is the best way to go. This Stealth Conversions' VSS unit comes in two styles: one for 34-39 tooth driven gears, and one for 40-45 tooth driven gears. They use the same speedometer gears as the Corvettes and Camaros. This unit will also trigger the 4-output vehicle speed buffer shown on page 12-2.

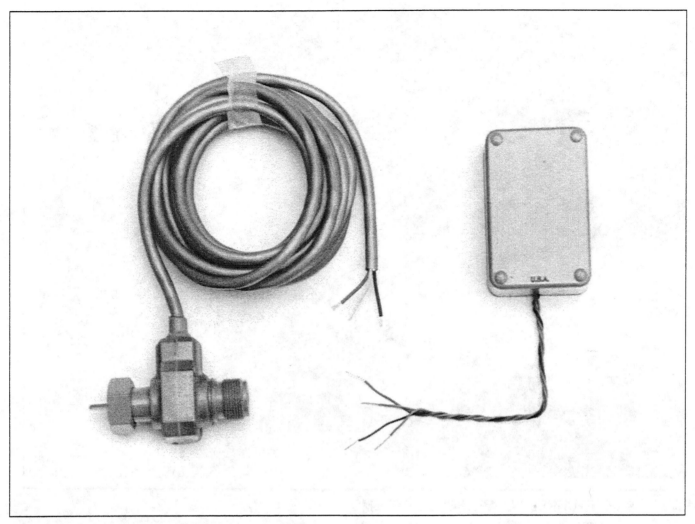

AFTERMARKET VEHICLE SPEED SENSORS

Stealth Conversions has several types of vehicle speed sensors designed for easy installation into vehicles that were not equipped with vehicle speed sensors, and electronic components to convert existing speed sensor or speedometer signals to be compatible with different engines.

Shown above are:

1. The two pulse unit used in all TBI installations, all computer controlled carbureted engines, and 1985-1989 TPI engines. The triggering mechanism is by Hall effect, and the unit has special electronics to work with the Chevrolet computer. Notice the heavy-duty shielded 18-gauge wire which protects against electrical noise and false triggering. This is a much more reliable unit than the reed switch units offered by some companies. It's like comparing point-type ignition to electronic ignition.

2. The pulse conditioner module for 1987 and newer trucks with electric speedometers that have 1990 and newer TPI engines. This unit taps off of the electrical speedometer signal and sends the proper signal to the 1990 and newer TPI ECM.

In addition to those shown above, Stealth Conversions has several other vehicle speed sensors for 1990 and newer TPI engines, and VSS conditioner modules for Jaguars with electric speedometers (1982 and newer). The Jaguar units tap off the Jaguar's electric speedometer, and send the proper signals to the Chevrolet ECMs. The California Air Resources Board (CARB) considers all of the Stealth Conversions VSS units as smog legal replacement parts for engine swaps.

TRANSMISSION TUNNEL CLEARANCE PROBLEMS

This is Stealth Conversions' 2-pulse vehicle speed sensor installed on a G-Body (1981 Malibu equipped with 700-R4 transmission). The length of the VSS required substantial floor pan modifications (we used a big hammer). Many vehicles (especially trucks) require no such modification.

There are several alternatives to this problem. One solution would be to run a 90° angle drive to angle the VSS away from the floor pan. Another solution would be to use a two-piece speedometer cable and install the VSS away from the transmission. Another solution would be to run the Stealth Conversions' VSS/speedometer sleeve (shown on page 12-4, and use it to trigger the 4-output VSS (shown on page 12-2) ECMs requiring a 2-pulse signal. Still another solution is to install the VSS on the cruise control module (if equipped) as shown on the next page.

When using a 1990 and newer TPI engine, use the Stealth Conversions' VSS/speedometer sleeve shown on page 12-4 (which only fits the 700-R4 transmission and Corvette six-speed ZF transmission). It installs in place of the normal speedometer sleeve, the speedometer cable screws onto it, and the factory 1990 and newer TPI wiring plugs into it.

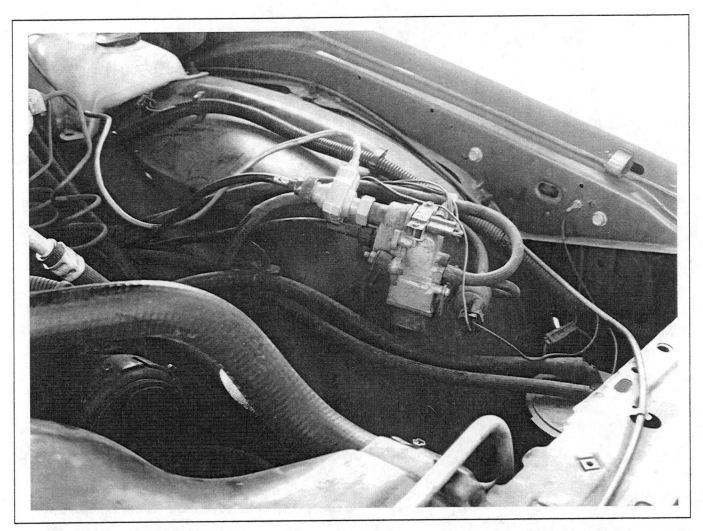

VSS MOUNTING OPTIONS

This is a variation of the short extension cable idea explained on the previous page. Here, the VSS is attached to the cruise control module to avoid transmission tunnel modifications.

The only problem with this type of VSS installation is if the speedometer cable is old and not lubricated properly. We have seen instances where the speedometer needle bounces at low vehicle speeds, and the computer reads the "bounces" and constantly locks and unlocks the torque converter. A lot of people think the transmission is damaged, but it is just a speedometer cable that needs lubrication or replacement. In more extreme cases, the "bouncing" speedometer cable will trigger the speed limiter (used in many new vehicles) which will temporarily cut fuel delivery to the engine resulting in a harsh jerking response.

SPEEDOMETER CALIBRATION

Calibrating the speedometer consists of using the appropriate speedometer gears in the transmission so that the speedometer cable turns 1000 revolutions in a mile. Some foreign cars have speedometers that require a different number of revolutions per mile, but it is usually close to 1000 revolutions per mile. If you look at the bottom of the speedometer face, it will often state the cable revolutions required per mile.

The above photo shows the speedometer drive gear and driven gear on a 700-R4 transmission. Numerous gears are available, and your Chevrolet dealer can supply the appropriate gears for your application.

If you are doing an engine swap into a non-Chevrolet vehicle and need a special speedometer cable, look in the Yellow Pages under "Speedometer". Most cities have speedometer shops that can make custom cables for under $50.

COOLING

The most common problem with engine swaps is overheating. A lot of the swaps do not overheat because of an inadequate radiator, they overheat due to insufficient air flow through the radiator. A lot of people think electric cooling fans are the "cure" for overheating problems. We believe that electric cooling fans are often the "cause" of overheating problems.

For example, a 1984 Camaro with a 4-cylinder engine comes with an electric cooling fan. The standard radiator for the 4-cylinder Camaro uses the same radiator core as a Chevrolet 1/2 ton full size truck with a 305 V8. The truck is heavier than the Camaro and has an engine that is literally twice the size, yet both come equipped with the same radiator core.

You would think that the truck would overheat with the "4-cylinder radiator core". The truck does not overheat because it uses an engine-driven cooling fan combined with a well designed fan shroud to effectively draw air through the radiator. The electric cooling fan in the Camaro cannot draw as much air through the radiator, and would be inadequate in the truck.

We do use and recommend electric cooling fans in a lot of applications, but you should know the limitations and drawbacks of electric cooling fans.

A lot of the electric cooling fans on the market do not cool an engine as well as their advertising would suggest. Quite simply, we have not seen an electric cooling fan that will move as much air through the radiator as a properly designed engine-driven fan and fan shroud. Electric fans have some advantages over engine-driven fans, but we generally try to stay away from them with vehicles that will be used for heavy towing.

FAN SHROUDS

When using an engine-driven fan, the correct fan shroud is an extremely important part of a properly functioning cooling system. The addition of a fan shroud to an engine-driven cooling fan can actually drop water temperature by as much as 60°F in many applications. A good way to test how well a fan is drawing air through the radiator is to place your hand in front of the radiator and feel if air is being drawn through. Often people will say, "the fan is blowing lots of air and my car still overheats." Sure, the fan may be blowing lots of air, but if you cannot feel it being drawn through the radiator, the car will overheat.

Ideally, a fan should be positioned 1/3 into the shroud. If the blades are completely enclosed within the shroud, the fan will not be as effective.

Due to the remote air cleaner used on most TPI installations, an engine-driven cooling fan cannot easily be used. Because of this, electric cooling fans are normally required. In some situations, trimming the fan shroud, and spacing the fan closer to the radiator may make enough room for the TPI air cleaner ducting. When spacers are used with a fan clutch, the weight of the fan clutch usually causes vibration problems. This is why Chevrolet does not use spacers with a fan clutch. When using a non-clutch fan, spacers do not cause a problem and are recommended for proper fan/fan-shroud positioning.

COOLING

ELECTRIC COOLING FANS, THEY MAY NOT BE ENOUGH!

Most electric cooling fans move air at about 12-15 mph. When driving down the road, cooling air is blocked and slowed down by the grille, bumper, and other obstructions in front of the radiator, including the electric cooling fans. So even though electric fans move air at only 12-15 mph, they are effective at greater vehicle speeds, but above 35-45 mph, they are virtually ineffective, unless there is a tail wind.

The biggest disadvantage of electric cooling fans is that the small electric motors just don't have the power to move air as well as an engine-driven cooling fan.

A typical 12" diameter electric cooling fan draws about 10 amps and is rated at 1000 cfm (cubic feet per minute). A 10 amp electric motor (at 12 volts) is making about 1/6 horsepower (120 watts). One horsepower equals 746 watts.

Tests from a magazine show that an 18" heavy-duty semi-flex fan draws about 1 horsepower at 2000 r.p.m. Assuming equal efficiencies, at 2000 r.p.m., the engine-driven fan draws about six times more air through the radiator than the typical 10 amp electric cooling fan. At 3500 r.p.m., the 18" fan requires 5 horsepower, but it is probably moving 30 times more air through the radiator as a 10 amp electric cooling fan. At 5000 r.p.m., the semi-flex fan draws about 9 horsepower. Tests from the same magazine article show that an engine-driven fan that uses a thermostatically controlled fan clutch draws less than 1 horsepower at almost any engine speed as long as the clutch engagement temperature is not exceeded.

Since most driving is done with the engine speed below 2000 r.p.m. (you are using an overdrive transmission, aren't you?), engine-driven cooling fans do not affect fuel mileage to a significant degree. When towing, engine speeds are generally higher (do not tow while in overdrive), so the fan does draw some horsepower, but the cooling air is usually necessary during towing conditions.

Because the power peak of most street V8 engines is below 5000 r.p.m., a typical 18" heavy-duty semi-flex cooling fan takes away about 9 horsepower at peak r.p.m., not the 15-20 that most companies advertise. A thermostatically-controlled clutch fan uses negligible horsepower when cold, and only requires about 5 horsepower at high engine speed when hot. If you can fit a thermostatically controlled clutch fan in your vehicle, use it because it is about the best thing going.

REVERSE PITCH FANS

Many of the fuel-injected engines use serpentine fan belts. Often, the water pump is driven backwards, compared to older engines. You cannot use a conventional fan in this situation because the fan will blow the air forward, and literally stop air flow through the radiator when the car is moving forward. If you have room for a fan clutch, make sure the fan clutch is designed for the reverse rotation fan. The late model Chevrolet Caprice and Chevrolet trucks and vans use reverse rotation fan blades and fan clutches. If you do not have space for a fan clutch, use the Flex-a-lite 1500 series engine-driven semi-flex fans. Model 1516 is 16" in diameter, 1517 is 17" diameter, 1518 is 18" diameter and 1519 is 19" diameter.

COOLING

ELECTRIC COOLING FANS, TIPS FOR BEST OPERATION

Electric cooling fans are now used in many car applications, mainly because most new cars are front-wheel-drive and have transversely-mounted engines that make using an engine-driven cooling fan impractical. As previously stated, electric cooling fans do not have the air flow capacity of an engine-driven fan. Most rear-wheel-drive V8 powered cars still use engine-driven cooling fans, the notable exceptions being Corvettes, Camaros, and Firebirds, which don't have much towing capacity. The standard 1994 Caprice uses electric cooling fans, but the towing package uses an engine-driven fan.

Electric cooling fans can do an excellent job of cooling, but electric fans must be chosen carefully and installed carefully for best results. There are several rules to adhere to when using electric cooling fans as primary cooling fans.

1. Use a sucker fan if possible.

2. Use the largest fan diameter to cover as much radiator surface as possible, or install two smaller fans if they will cover more radiator surface area.

3. Use a fan with the highest amperage rating.

4. Use a good radiator.

It is important to use the fan as it is designed to be used. A **sucker** (or puller) fan is designed to be mounted behind the radiator where it sucks air through the radiator. A **pusher** fan is designed to be mounted in front of the radiator where it pushes air through the radiator.

Most importantly, a fan should be mounted so that the convex part of the fan blade is facing forward. Mounting a fan so that the convex part of the blade faces rearward will substantially reduce the amount of air that the fan can move.

Some fans can be used as either sucker or pusher fans, i.e., the fans can be removed from the electric motor and installed facing the other direction.

Without a doubt, a sucker fan is more effective at cooling than an equally rated pusher fan. It is our opinion that a sucker fan rated at 1000 c.f.m. will cool as well as a pusher fan rated at 1500 c.f.m. If you have room behind the radiator for a sucker fan, by all means, use a sucker fan.

Use the largest fan diameter possible to get the best radiator coverage. If you can get better radiator coverage by using two smaller fans, use two smaller fans, rather than one big fan.

Use a fan with the highest amperage draw. Assuming that most electric cooling fan motors have equal efficiencies, the fan that has a higher current draw can move the most air.

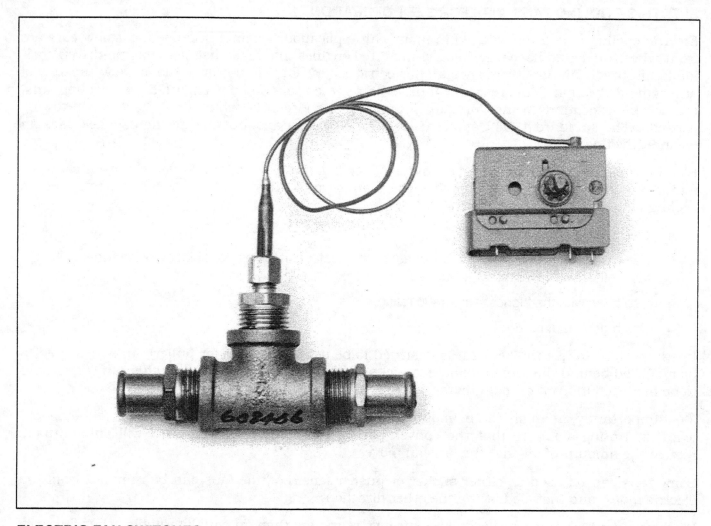

ELECTRIC FAN SWITCHES

Flex-a-lite makes an adjustable temperature switch that is designed to be installed into the upper radiator hose using a rubber sleeve or grommet. It is adjustable from 180-240°F. We have been using the Flex-a-lite model for years and they have been very reliable. A street-rodder showed us a better way to install the Flex-a-lite unit by using parts from the hardware store. It requires using a 1/4" brass compression fitting with a 1/2" N.P.T. male end. The compression fitting assembly (minus the brass o-ring) is drilled through with a 17/64" drill bit so that the temperature probe can be installed as shown.

The compression fitting adapter is then installed into the heater hose using a 1/2" N.P.T. "T" and two 5/8" x 1/2" N.P.T. heater hose nipples.

A coolant shut-off valve is not used in many vehicles. Engine coolant constantly circulates through the heater core, so this type of temperature switch works great in those vehicles. On vehicles that use a heater shut-off valve, this temperature switch installation will not work when the shut-off valve is closed unless a bypass hose is installed.

RADIATOR DESIGNS

There are a lot of different radiator designs, and different materials: Copper-brass, aluminum, 1-row core, 2-row core, 3-row core, 4-row core, continuous fin, louvered fin, straight fin, serpentine fin, dimpled tube, cross flow, down flow, high efficiency core, 1-pass core, 2-pass core... etc.

A lot of the different designs have more to do with marketing strategies than actual cooling ability.

On the left is a one-row aluminum radiator core used on the TPI Camaro. The tube width is 1-1/4" and the tubes are spaced at 7/16" intervals. The Camaro radiator uses louvered serpentine fins, with a fin density of 20 fins/inch. It is a very efficient radiator and is designed to be used with electric cooling fans.

The center radiator core is a two-row copper-brass design that is used on a lot of cars built in the early 1980s. The tubes are 3/8" wide and they are spaced at 7/16" intervals. Fin density is typically 14-16 fins/inch.

The core on the right is also a two-row copper-brass design. Its tubes are 1/2" wide and they are spaced a 9/16" intervals. This design was used through the 1970s. Fin density is typically 12-14 fins/inch.

The one-row core on the left is the best cooling and lightest weight of the three radiators shown above. Due to the width of its tubes, the fin design, the fin density, and the excellent fin-to-tube contact area, it outperforms most 3-row radiators and even some 4-row radiators.

COOLING

As you can see, there is a lot more to radiators than core thickness or the number of rows of tubes.

Generally, we always try to use a plastic/aluminum GM radiator if a suitable one exists for the application because of their light weight, low cost, and excellent cooling capabilities. We have actually solved cooling problems in some cars by replacing so called "heavy duty" 3-row radiators with the one-row plastic/aluminum radiators.

From an environmental standpoint, the plastic/aluminum radiator is considered safer than a copper/brass radiator, which contains lead solder. The lead will actually get into the coolant. In some states, ethylene glycol is not considered a hazardous waste, but "used" antifreeze is, because of the lead content. The plastic side tanks are recyclable, as is the aluminum core.

The plastic/aluminum radiators have been very reliable. The plastic tanks seem to have a service life of only about 5–7 years on vehicles which consistenly run at temperatures above 220°F, but we have not experienced any problems on vehicles that rarely exceed 205°F. The plastic tanks can be replaced by most modern radiator shops for a reasonable fee. Our biggest caution is that the radiator hoses should be carefully fitted so that there is no stress on the inlet or outlet. On vehicles with automatic transmissions, the cooler lines should be carefully adjusted so that there is no strain where they connect to the radiator.

For ultra-heavy-duty cooling, we order custom made radiators with a 4-row core using 1/2" wide tubes that are spaced 7/16" between tube centers, and we specify that it have 14 fins/inch. The fin design we specify is the louvered serpentine design. The core thickness is 2-5/8". We also specify a heavy duty transmission oil cooler inside the radiator tank (see next page) when using an automatic transmission. Most good radiator shops can custom build radiators to your specifications. Expect to pay about $400 for the ultra-heavy-duty customs.

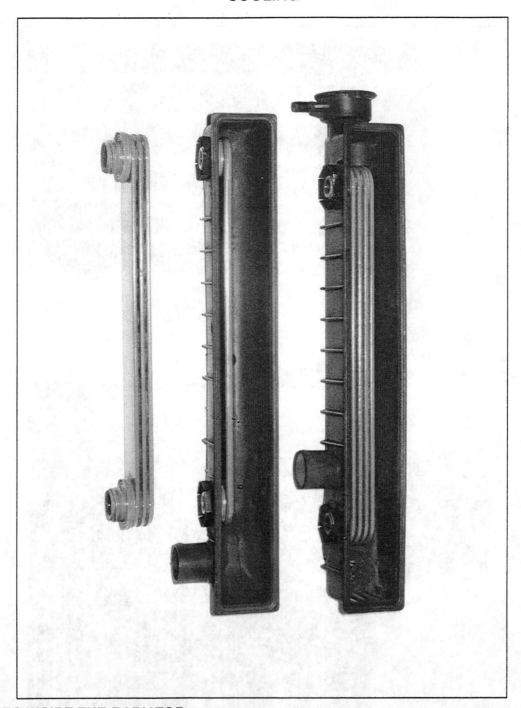

OIL COOLERS INSIDE THE RADIATOR

There are different types of oil coolers mounted inside radiators. There are both engine oil coolers and transmission oil coolers, and they both come with different cooling capacities.

On the left is a 3-plate engine oil cooler. It has fittings that accommodate 1/2" hose or tubing. Transmission oil coolers typically use 5/16" hose or tubing. Never use a transmission oil cooler to cool engine oil because the restricted oil flow will destroy the engine.

In the center is a 1-plate transmission oil cooler installed in a radiator side tank. On the right is a 4-plate transmission oil cooler mounted in the radiator tank.

If you are going to have a custom-made heavy-duty radiator built for your engine swap and you plan on towing, or using a high-stall speed torque converter, you should specify a heavy-duty 4 or 5-plate transmission cooler so that you wont need to install an external transmission oil cooler.

RADIATOR FIN DESIGN

This shows two different radiator fin designs. The (slightly beat up) radiator on top has a conventional serpentine fin design. The radiator on the bottom has a "continuous" or "straight" fin design. The continuous fin core is more resistant to vibration and stone damage, and is often used in diesel trucks and off-road vehicles.

The serpentine fin is better at cooling than the continuous fin design.

We mention this because a lot of radiator shops mistakenly think the continuous-fin radiator is the "HOT" set-up.

COOLING

ENGINE OIL COOLERS AND SYNTHETIC OILS

Engine oil coolers are rarely needed in most passenger cars, but are recommended for engines which are used at high speeds for long periods of time.

The engineers who designed the LT1 engine for the 1992 Corvette got away from using an engine oil cooler simply by specifying synthetic oil for the engine. Remember, the Corvette LT1 is designed for extreme use. Corvettes are designed to compete in showroom stock racing with no modifications other than safety equipment. The synthetic oils can handle much higher temperatures than conventional oils without losing lubricating qualities. The engineers learned that it would be less expensive to use synthetic oils than to install an auxiliary oil cooler. Another benefit of not using an engine oil cooler is that there are less parts to break, and less connections to leak.

We have been using Redline synthetic lubricants in our vehicles for years with excellent results. The synthetics have proven cost effective for us because we double the mileage between oil change intervals and our engines show no wear. In addition, we add oil less often between changes. We attribute this to the synthetic oil's higher vaporization temperature; the synthetic oils remains a liquid on the cylinder walls when the conventional oils have already evaporated off of the cylinder walls and into the combustion gases.

COOLING TIPS AND RECOMMENDATIONS

For vehicles that are having a cooling problem in hot weather we recommend using less antifreeze (ethylene glycol) and more water. Using less anti-freeze to improve cooling is no secret. Chevrolet recommends only a 45% mixture of anti-freeze in American S-10 Trucks, but recommends 50% in Canadian S-10 Trucks. Chevrolet recommends 50% anti-freeeze in most of its other cars and trucks sold in America. Water is a better coolant than ethylene glycol—it has a lower viscosity and flows through the engine better, it also absorbs heat better.

The problem with using pure water is that it does not offer protection against corrosion, and it freezes at 32°F. Red Line (known for their synthetic lubricants) has a radiator coolant additive that protects against corrosion even when using no antifreeze. The additive, however, will not lower the freezing point of the coolant. The greater percentage of water will reduce coolant temperatures. On our vehicles that are prone to running hot (V8 S-10 trucks, for example), we will run a 25% mixture of anti-freeze with a bottle of Red Line rust and corrosion inhibitor in the summer. In the winter, we run a 50% mixture of antifreeze for freezing protection. Checking the mixture is easily done with a hydrometer for radiator coolant. Hydrometers are available at most auto parts stores for less than $10. Many "racers" use water soluble oil in their race cars instead of anti-freeze to provide protection against corrosion. However, the water soluble oils quickly deteriorate rubber radiator hoses. Water soluble oils are not suitable for use in street cars.

During hard usage, the elimination of hot spots can be more important than reducing coolant temperature. The 1992 Chevrolet Corvette LT1 went to reverse flow cooling to improve engine cooling. The reverse flow cooling offers many benefits, however, the reverse flow cooling does not actually lower coolant temperatures. It does reduce hot spots in the engine, which allows the ignition timing to be advanced because of reduced detonation sensitivity in the cylinders that would otherwise suffer from hot spots. The Red Line coolant additive and reduced concentration of anti-freeze (ethylene glycol) is one way to reduce hot spots — this is highly recommended for vehicles that run hot.

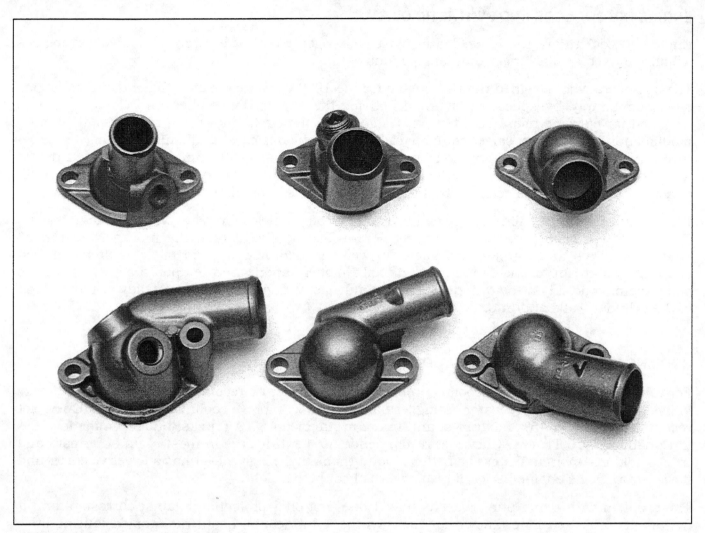

THERMOSTAT HOUSINGS

Thermostat housings come in a variety of styles. All of the above are for the Chevrolet V8. Some have provisions for thermostatically controlled switches or sending units. If you need something special for your vehicle, look in an Everco or Four-Seasons catalog. Most automotive parts stores carry Everco or Four-Seasons parts.

The TPI thermostat housing makes it difficult to run an engine-driven fan. To provide clearance for an engine-driven fan on TPI engines, we modify the TPI thermostat housing by cutting and welding the outlet so that it is pointed straight out to the left of the engine, or we install the thermostat housing from a 1988–1992 Camaro 305 TBI (shown on lower right), which allows running the hose out the side of the engine, away from the engine-driven fan (see TPI Volvo on page 1–10).

IN-LINE HOSE FILLERS

In many engine swaps, a conventional radiator filler neck is not possible due to clearance reasons. To add coolant, an in-line radiator hose filler is the only practical solution. Without a pressure relief cap, serious problems can develop in the cooling system. Moroso makes several in-line hose fillers which are readily available at many auto parts stores or through mail-order outfits. A good radiator shop can also make an in-line hose filler.

The top left in-line hose filler is Moroso part #63730. It fits 1-1/2" radiator hoses.

The top right in-line hose filler is Moroso part #63754. It fits 1-1/4" radiator hoses.

The lower in-line hose filler, Moroso part #63740, fits 1-1/2" hose on one end and 1-1/4" hose on the other end.

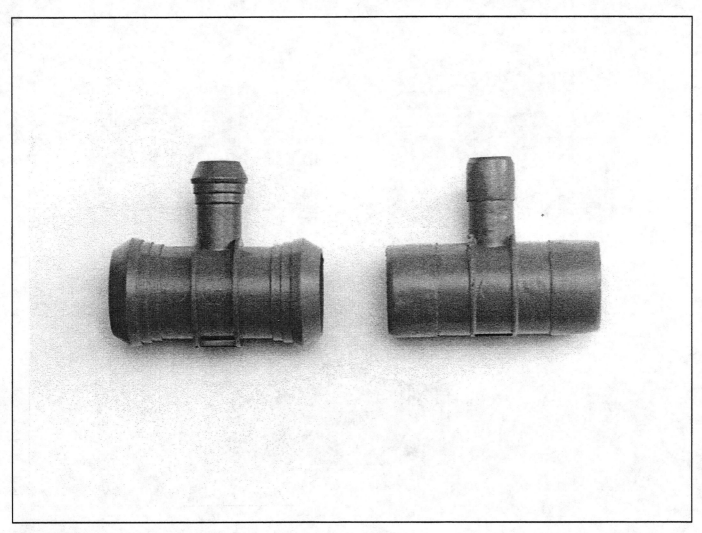

TEE TIME

If you are using a TBI or TPI engine that has only one heater hose fitting on the engine, and the radiator in your vehicle has no provisions for connecting the heater hose return, Stealth Conversions offers a tee that installs into the lower radiator hose so that the radiator can remain stock.

The tees are made of high-strength plastic and are designed for 1-3/4" diameter radiator hoses, and 7/8" heater hose. The tee on the right has been modified by filing or grinding the ridges off so that it can be used for 1-1/2" radiator hose and 3/4" heater hose.

Do not install the tee into the upper radiator hose because the coolant will go through the radiator, bypassing the thermostat.

HEATER HOSE FITTINGS AND COOLING EFFICIENCY

The three heater hose fittings are all for 5/8" hose and all have 1/2" npt (national pipe thread).

The fitting on the left is a standard unit which has a 7/16" opening (Everco part #H805).

The center fitting (Everco part #4894) has a restriction. Its opening is only 3/8". The stock TPI and TBI heater hose fittings have a similar restriction.

The fitting on the right is Everco part #H4894, but the inside diameter has been further restricted by threading it with a 1/8" npt tap and installing a 1/8" pipe nipple. The excess pipe nipple was cut off with a hacksaw. The opening is 1/4" and has proven adequate for coolant flow to the heater. GM part #10039163 (used on 1985-1992 2.5 liter Chevrolet S-10 Trucks) has a similar restriction. Retail cost is less than $4.

In applications with the Stealth Conversions' tee in the lower radiator hose, the restricted heater hose fitting has noticeably improved engine cooling by causing more coolant to be pulled through the radiator, and less through the heater core.

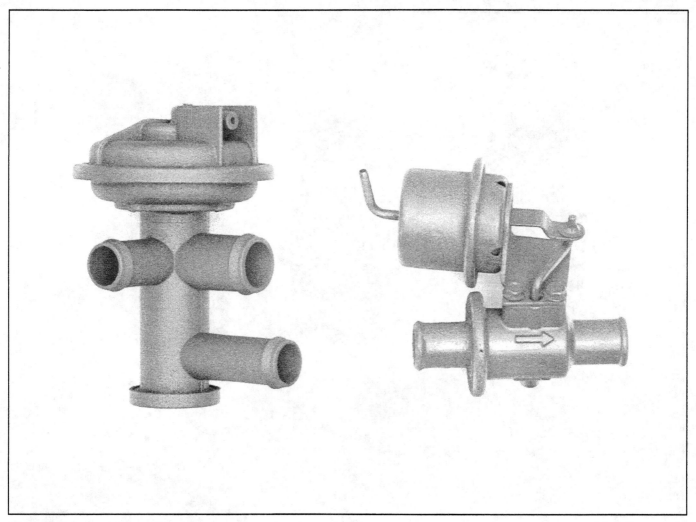

HEATER HOSE VALVES

On the left is the coolant *bypass* valve used on 1987-1992 Camaros equipped with air conditioning. When the air conditioning is on "MAX Cooling," coolant is *diverted* from going through the heater core, but coolant still flows through the throttle body on TPI engines to prevent "icing" of the throttle blades, and through the oil cooler (if equipped). The bypass valve requires a tee in the heater hose return line (see next page). Look in the Camaro shop manual under "Air Conditioning" for proper hose routing.

The coolant *shut-off* valve on the right (from a 1981 El Camino with air conditioning) *stops* coolant flow when the air conditioning is on "MAX Cooling."

TBI engines can use the shut-off valve, and simplify heater hose plumbing because TBI engines use thermostatically controlled air cleaners which preheat the intake air to prevent icing.

The above valves bypass or stop coolant flow when vacuum is applied, but other valves are available that stop or bypass coolant when no vacuum is applied. Everco and Four-Seasons catalogs (available in most auto parts stores) have listings of various valves that will meet your requirements.

Many vehicles do not have coolant bypass or shut-off valves. However, not installing a valve on a vehicle designed for such a valve can impair air conditioning performance. We have solved numerous complaints of poor air conditioning performance on Chevrolet powered Jaguars by installing the proper coolant valve.

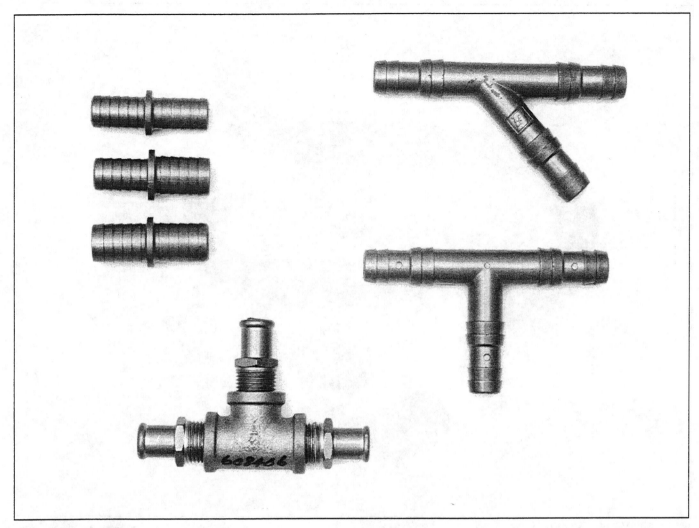

HEATER HOSES

In some conversions, it is necessary to join a 5/8" heater hose to a 3/4" hose. The fittings on the upper left are Goodyear heater hose splicers. The top splicer is for 5/8" to 5/8" (Goodyear part #65095). The center splice is 5/8" to 3/4" (Goodyear part #65097). The bottom splicer is for 3/4" to 3/4" hose (Goodyear part #65096). Goodyear hoses and splicers are available at many auto parts stores. Goodyear also has specially molded 90° heater hoses that can be connected with the splicers shown above for custom installations.

For vehicles with heater bypass valves, and/or oil coolers that use engine coolant as the cooling medium, a "tee" is often needed so that coolant will circulate properly through the engine and oil cooler when the heater is shut off.

The bottom tee was made using a 1/2" plumbing tee at the hardware store, and heater hose fittings.

The fittings on the top right are Everco #3875 (top) and Everco #H3841 (lower). These tees will accommodate 5/8" and 3/4" heater hoses. The tees are made of high quality plastic.

For real difficult heater hose routing, Cool-Flex™ heater hose from Total Performance can be used. It is a flexible ribbed chrome plated copper tube that is easily bent to fit almost any configuration. It stays in the the desired shape, while still being flexible enough to allow for normal engine movement. The Cool-Flex™ heater hose is a super product for engine swaps and is available at many street-rod shops and through mail-order shops.

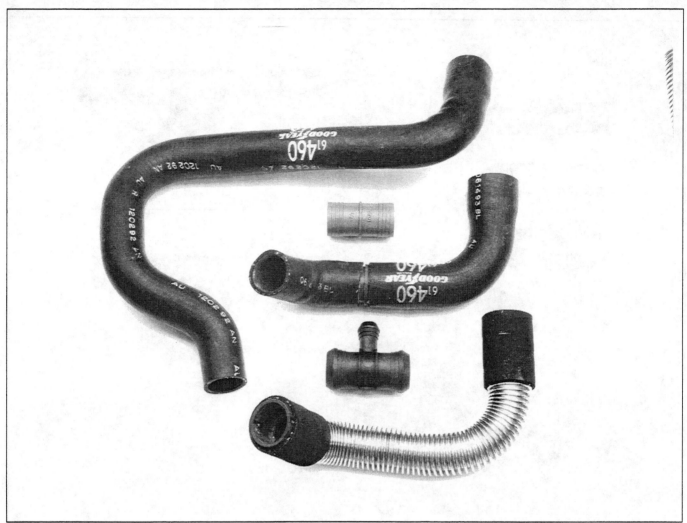

RADIATOR HOSE TIPS

On some engine swaps, getting a molded radiator hose to fit your particular application can be next to impossible. We have often cut and spliced different sections of radiator hoses to fit the swap. Even so, on some swaps, this can be time consuming, and the hose still seems to contact something.

For example, on S-10 Truck V8 conversions, we will cut and splice a molded hose to make the lower radiator hose. If the engine has no provisions for a heater hose return, we will use the Stealth Conversions' Tee to join the two sections of hose.

Generally, we refrain from flex-hose because of various problems we have had, such as the wire spring popping through the hose and leaking, and the stress a flex hose can put on radiator fittings can cause radiators to leak (especially the plastic/aluminum radiators).

A great product that can be used when a specially shaped radiator hose is required is Cool-Flex™ made by Total Performance (shown on the bottom). This is a flexible ribbed chrome plated copper tube that can be bent to the required shape. It stays in that shape while still being flexible enough to allow for normal engine movement without putting stress on the radiator fittings. The ends of the Cool-Flex™ connect to the engine and radiator with 1-3/4" rubber hose end (and reducer bushings for 1-1/2" and 1-1/4" fittings). Billet style ends are also available to dress up the engine compartment. Cool-Flex™ is available at many street-rod shops and through mail-order shops.

AIR CONDITIONING

With engine swaps, one confusing item with the air conditioning is when the vehicle uses an "expansion valve" system and the TPI/TBI engine came out of a vehicle with a cycling clutch system. The important thing to remember is that the vehicle's air conditioning will control the compressor on the engine. All automotive air conditioning compressor's work on the same principles-they compress freon. If you are installing a TPI engine (which came out of a vehicle that uses a cycling clutch system) into a Jaguar (which uses an expansion valve system), simply connect the Jaguar's air conditioning wire to the Chevrolet compressor. The Jaguar's air conditioning controls will operate the compressor's clutch.

The **real** confusing part of the air conditioning is installing and wiring the high pressure safety switches and cooling fan switches to protect the air conditioning system against excessive temperatures and pressures.

Camaro fuel-injected engines have the compressor high pressure shut-off switch attached directly to the compressor, and the switch is wired into the engine harness. You should not have to add, or connect any additional wires to make the high pressure shut-off switch functional.

Corvette TPI engines are different. The high-pressure shut-off switch is connected to the hose on the high-pressure side of the system. You will have to install and wire the high-pressure shut-off switch onto your vehicle if you are using a Corvette air conditioning compressor.

If you are not running an engine-driven cooling fan, the electric cooling fans should be controlled by the air conditioning system. Most of the TPI engines have the electric cooling fans operated by a pressure switch on the high-pressure side of the air conditioning system. The electric cooling fans are also controlled by vehicle speed. Above a certain speed (normally about 40 m.p.h.), the fans are turned off because the vehicle will have enough air going through the condenser to cool properly. The fan operation is explained in the factory shop manual (available from Helm). The wiring is also shown in the factory shop manual.

Most of the TBI engines activate the fans whenever the air conditioning is turned on. For most people, it will be easier to wire the electric cooling fans to operate whenever the air conditioning is turned on. The information on wiring the fans is in the factory shop manual.

IMPORTANT! Check that the wiring is correct by disconnecting the wiring to the high-pressure shut-off switch to see if the compressor clutch disengages. Do the same for the low-pressure switch.

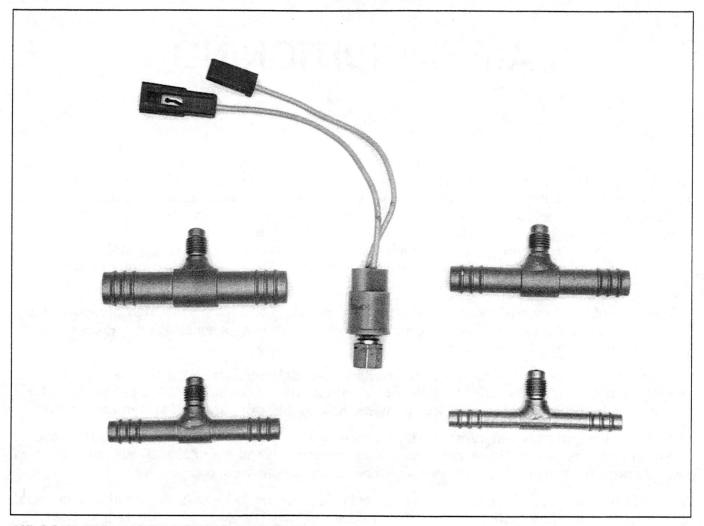

AIR CONDITIONING PRESSURE SWITCHES

At the time of this writing, no hose splicers were available that could be used with the factory Chevrolet air conditioning pressure switches.

The above fittings are hose splicers with charging valves. They all use a 1/4" male SAE flare thread for the service port. The hose splicers shown are for hoses ranging from #6 (5/16") to #12 (5/8").

The pressure switch shown in the center installs on the 1/4" SAE flare service port, and can be used to control the electric cooling fans, and/or the compressor high-pressure shut-off. The switch is available for many different applications: Normally open, normally closed, and with activation pressures ranging from 10 psi to over 400 psi. Four-Seasons, Everco, and NAPA carry these switches.

When ordering pressure switches for your vehicle, be sure to check the pressure range you need, and be sure to check if the switch is normally open or normally closed. The information for your engine is available in the factory shop manual (available from Helm), in the electrical section for "Air conditioning" and in the section for "Electric cooling fan."

Don't worry about getting a switch with the exact pressures as in the factory shop manual, but do get a switch that is relatively close (within 25 psi) to the factory specifications.

Eventually, hose splicers will be available with the correct O-ring fittings that the Chevrolet switches require, which will allow the use of the factory pressure switches.

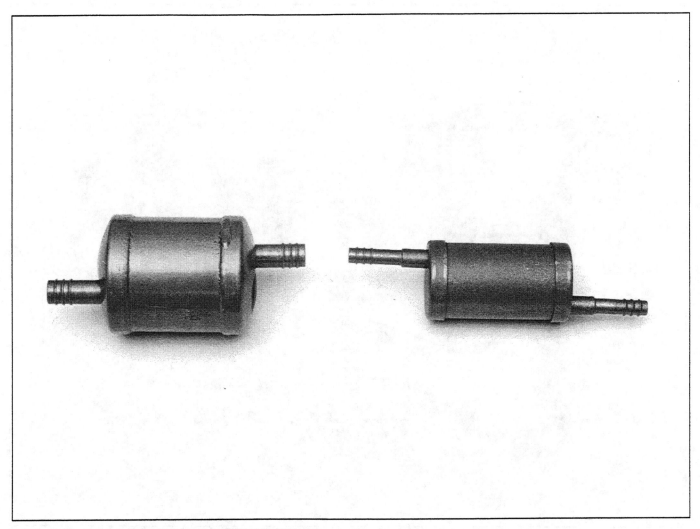

MUFFLERS FOR AIR CONDITIONING NOISES

In many engine swaps, an air conditioning muffler is required to quiet the pulsations caused by the air conditioning compressor. If you hear a buzzing or humming sound that varies with engine speed only when the air conditioning is turned on, you may want to install a muffler in your air conditioning hose to quiet the noise. Normally, a muffler is installed on the high-pressure side. In some cases, two mufflers are needed; one on the high side, and one on the low side.

Cars with the air conditioning evaporator mounted inside the car (many foreign cars) are more likely to have the noise problem than vehicles with the evaporator mounted in the engine compartment (most Chevrolet vehicles have the evaporator mounted in the engine compartment).

Mufflers are available in many different configurations and sizes. Four-Seasons, NAPA, and Everco, all carry numerous air conditioning mufflers. Most automotive air-conditioning shops (in the Yellow Pages under "Automotive Air Conditioning Equipment-Service and Repair") can easily install mufflers into your vehicle.

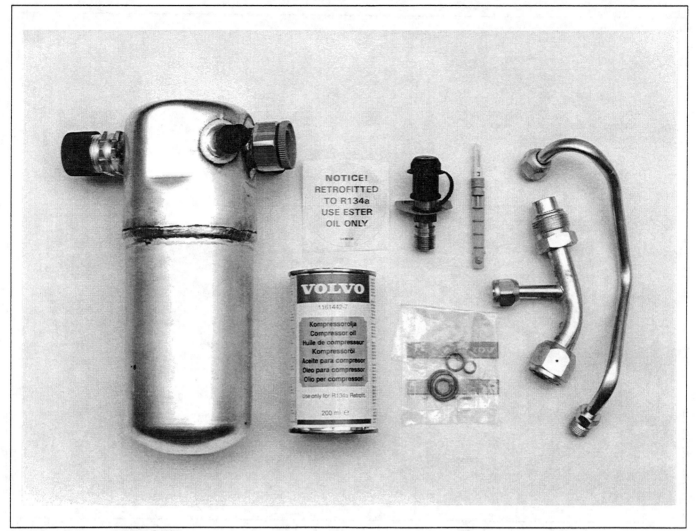

FREON R134a RETROFIT

Freon 12 will be unavailable in the next few years because it is depleting the ozone layer that filters the sun's harmful rays. In the future, you will have to convert your vehicle's air conditioning system to Freon R134a if your air conditioning needs recharged.

Volvo already has a retrofit kit for some of its models. The kit consists of a new accumulator, a new orifice tube, new o-rings, special filling valves, special oil, and a sticker to show that the system has been converted to R134a. The kit is priced at about $125 as shown and is not difficult to install.

The reason we are showing the Volvo[1] kit is that Volvo uses GM air-conditioning parts, and we believe that GM has kits for its vehicles. Most likely, Volvo has gotten the parts to market sooner than GM because Volvo is a much smaller company that GM.

Other parts not in the kit that may be required are barrier type air-conditioning hoses, and a pressure cycling switch that is calibrated for R134a. Goodyear "Galaxy" air-conditioning hoses are compatible with R134a, and are readily available at most auto parts stores that carry air-conditioning parts.

---

1. Did you know that JTR's *Volvo 200 Series V8 Conversion Manual* should be available in June, 1994? That's the real reason we are showing the Volvo kit!

POWER STEERING

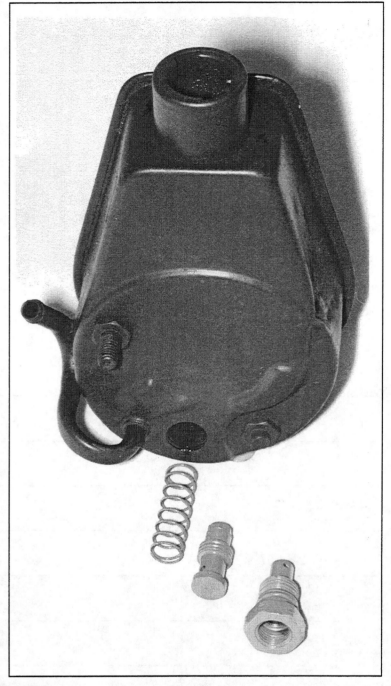

The power steering pumps used on the fuel injected engines use an O-ring fitting (left photo, upper fitting) for the high pressure power steering hose. If you are installing a TPI/TBI engine into your older GM vehicle that uses an inverted flare (left photo, bottom fitting) on the high pressure hose, you can replace the union, pressure relief valve, and spring from the pump (shown removed from the pump) that originally came with the car so that the original power steering hose can be used and the pressure relief valve is correct for the steering system in your vehicle.

If you are installing your engine into a non-GM car which uses different hose fittings, a hydraulic hose shop can make a hose for your application. To find a shop near you, look in the Yellow Pages under "Hydraulic Equipment and Supplies."

Generally, most power steering pumps on TPI/TBI engines put out a maximum of 1000–1200 PSI on Camaros, to 1250–1500 PSI on Corvettes, and are compatible with most other power steering systems.

To make sure that the pressures for the steering pump and steering box (or rack) are compatible, check your shop manuals in the power steering chapter. If you need to lower the pressure relief, the spring in the pressure relief valve can be trimmed down a bit, or exchanged for one with a lower rating. More information on the pump is available in the factory shop manual (available from Helm).

POWER STEERING
Note Page

CALIFORNIA SMOG LAWS

DON'T WORRY, THEY AREN'T THAT BAD!

Due to some mis-information, and exageration; people across the country think the California style smog laws are the end of engine swaps. Even in California, many automotive enthusiasts beleive it against the law to perform engine swaps. Engine swaps are still allowed in California, and the laws regarding engine swaps have been the same since 1984.

The *basic intent* of the California engine change laws is that when you do an engine swap, the new engine/transmission cannot pollute more than the original engine/transmission. This means the newly installed engine must be the same year (or newer) as the vehicle, and all emissions controls on the newly installed engine must be installed and functional. Also, you can't put a truck engine into a car, or a heavy-duty truck engine into a light-duty truck because light-duty trucks have less stringent emissions limits than cars, and heavy-duty trucks have even less stringent emissions limits than light-duty trucks.

To get your engine swap approved, you must go to a *Referee Station*. The Referee Inspection is free, and it is a benefit for people who do smog-legal engine changes because the engine change can be approved on a visual inspection, current smog laws, and common sense.

The Referee inspector will check the engine to be sure it is the same year (or newer) as the vehicle and then inspect the engine/transmission and chassis for all the proper smog equipment. If all is there, an "Engine Identification" tag will be placed in the door jamb. The "Engine Identification" tag is not mentioned on any registration papers or ownership papers. It is only on the vehicle.

If your vehicle does not pass the visual inspection, and you feel it should, you can have the Referee Inspector call the engineering office for a ruling. If the engineering office fails your vehicle and you think it should pass, you can always run it through the California Air Resources Board (CARB) for a full Federal Test Procedure (FTD), but that can cost you several thousand dollars, and your vehicle may still fail. Remember, the Referee Inspection program is a benefit for people who do engine swaps.

People who understand smog controls and how they work usually have no problems with the Referee Station. People who don't understand how smog controls work are the ones who tend to have difficulties with the smog laws.

The California smog laws on engine swaps (or engine changes) are consistent with common sense, safety, and emissions reduction. The laws are fair and necessary. We cannot think of a better and fairer way to keep *our* air clean.

The EPA recognizes California smog laws as being applicable across the nation: That is, if it is legal in California, then according to the EPA, it is legal in all other states. Other States will be adopting the California smog laws because there has been a tremendous amount of time and money invested in making the California smog laws reasonable, consistent, and effective for pollution reduction. It is far cheaper for other state governments to adopt the California laws rather than come up with their own laws. When the smog laws are consistent across the nation, there will be far less confusion for all involved.

BUY THE BOOK

For the best information on smog laws in California, go to your local Bureau of Automotive Repair (BAR) office, and purchase the *Smog Check Inspection Manual*. To find one near you, look in the phone book in the "State Government Offices" section, under "Automotive Repair Bureau".

The inspection manual costs less than $10 and is filled with valuable information.

CALIFORNIA SMOG LAWS

THE INSPECTION PROCEDURE

Let's assume you have done a California smog-legal engine change to your vehicle. You have installed an engine that is the same year (or newer) as your vehicle, with all of the required smog equipment and controls for both the engine and transmission. The newly installed engine is not a truck engine into a car, or a heavy-duty truck engine into a light-duty truck. The chassis has the correct emissions controls: Catalytic converter, charcoal canister, and fuel filler restrictor (if required). Your next step is to visit a "referee station." If you simply want to know what is required to be smog legal, purchase the *Smog Check Inspection Manual* as explained on the previous page. If the manual does not explain what you need to know, call one of the phone numbers listed in the *Smog Check Inspection Manual.*

The DMV (Department of Motor Vehicles) can get you the phone number required to make an appointment with the referee station. When you call to make the appointment, the person on the phone will ask you why you need to go to the referee station. Your answer will be, "Engine change." If you say, "Engine swap" or "V8 conversion," the person on the phone may not know what you are talking about, so please, just say "engine change."

Next, the person will ask for your name, address, and the vehicle's license number. You will then get an appointment date, which can range anywhere from the very next day, to five weeks away. Some areas have appointments on Saturdays if that is more convenient for you. Within a few days, you will receive a postcard in the mail confirming your appointment date, and it will tell you to bring the vehicle's registration papers and any other smog-related paperwork that you may have.

When you arrive at the referee station, be polite, be honest, and be patient. The inspectors rarely see engine swaps. They usually see stock vehicles that have failed the smog inspection. The inspectors are a lot like police officers—they are highly trained, and the public only sees them when there is a problem. Remember, it is their job to make sure your vehicle is smog legal. For all they know, you could be an undercover inspector, so don't expect the inspector to let anything slide, because his job may be at stake.

The inspectors have a general training in smog inspection, and will not necessarily be an expert on the type of engine in your car. They see Volkswagens, Jaguars, Volkswagens, Fords, Volkswagens, Chryslers, Volkswagens, Datsuns, Volkswagens, Toyotas, Volkswagens, Mercedes, Volkswagens, Chevrolets, and Volkswagens—just about everything ever built, so they cannot be expected to be an expert on every vehicle's smog equipment, unless of course it's a Volkswagen.

The inspection takes anywhere from 30 minutes to over one hour, depending on the inspector and the type of "engine change." Some inspectors will want to be left alone with your vehicle, others may ask for your assistance in locating devices such as the charcoal canister, vehicle speed sensor, or the wiring for the lock-up torque converter. The inspector will check ignition timing and EGR operation.

If your vehicle passes the visual inspection, a sticker will be placed in the door jamb or engine compartment (see next page).

If your vehicle does not pass the visual inspection, you will be given a form explaining what your vehicle will need to pass the inspection. You will need to correct the problem(s) listed on the form and make another appointment with the referee station.

After the visual inspection, the vehicle will be given the tailpipe (or sniffer) test. The tailpipe test is quite lenient. If your vehicle cannot pass the tailpipe test, something is wrong, or your engine has been modified a lot. Generally, a vehicle's tail pipe emissions will be about 1/3 of the allowable standards if it is running decently.

CALIFORNIA SMOG LAWS

If your vehicle passes the visual inspection and the tail pipe test, you will get the smog inspection certificate ($7 fee) so that you can register your vehicle. The certificate has no indication of the "engine change," and is the same type of certificate that "normal" vehicles receive for passing the inspection.

If your vehicle passes the visual inspection, but does not pass the tailpipe test, you will still get the "Engine identification" sticker because the referee station does not want to see you again. You will be required to get your vehicle inspected at a "normal" smog inspection station. "Normal" smog inspection stations charge about $40 for a smog inspection, so you really want your vehicle to pass the tailpipe test at the Referee Station.

CALIFORNIA SMOG LAWS

We at JTR really do believe in running clean cars. We are located in a high smog area and we see (and smell) the smog in the air almost every day. Now that we have the technology to make cars perform well and run clean, lets make an effort to keep OUR air clean.

The sticker in the door jamb (below) allows the car to be subsequently tested at any smog inspection station. It gives the following information on what smog equipment the vehicle requires.

VIN No.– Serial number of the vehicle
YR. – Year of the engine (not the vehicle)
SIZE – Engine size
MFG – Manufacturer of the engine
F/C – Federal/California smog requirements
M/A – Manual/Automatic transmission
SITE – Where the car was inspected
B/A – Before/After. If the engine was installed before March of 1984, it may not need any smog controls
NOX – NOx Emissions Controls
PCV – Positive Crankcase Ventilation

TAC – Thermostatic Air Cleaner
AIS – Air Injection System
EVP – Evaporative Controls (charcoal canister)
FR – Fuel Filler Restrictor (unleaded gas)
OC – Oxidizing Catalytic Converter
TWC – Three-Way Catalytic Converter
EGR – Exhaust Gas Recirculation
SPK – Spark (distributor) controls
COM – Computer
C/I – Carburetor/Injection
OTH – Other smog controls

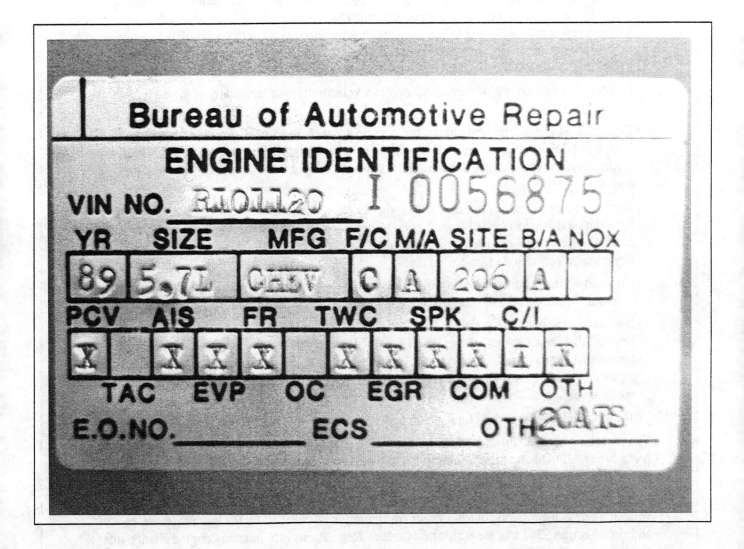

Bureau of Automotive Repair
ENGINE IDENTIFICATION
VIN NO. R101120   I 0056875

YR	SIZE	MFG	F/C	M/A	SITE	B/A	NOX
89	5.7L	CHEV	C	A	206	A	

PCV		AIS	FR	TWC		SPK		C/I	
X		X	X	X		X	X	X	X

TAC   EVP   OC   EGR   COM   OTH

E.O.NO. _____   ECS _____   OTH 2CATS

This is the latest information regarding California engine swap laws (dated January, 1993) as presented by the State of California Department of Consumer Affairs.

Guidelines for Performing Legal Engine Changes

Engine changes continue to present problems and challenges to car owners and technicians. Here are some tips to keep you and your customers on the straight and narrow.

Our recommendation is to rebuild and reinstall the original engine/transmission and emission control configuration. When rebuilding an engine it must be rebuilt to the original equipment specifications. However, if you do decide to change the engine, the following guidelines must be observed to ensure that the vehicle will be eligible for smog certification or registration:

• Make sure the engine and emission control configuration on exhaust-controlled vehicles are certified to the year of the vehicle or newer, and to the same or a more stringent new vehicle certification standard.

• Voiding the vehicle manufacturer's emission warranty will not be allowed.

• Mixing and matching emission control system components could cause problems and is generally not allowed. Engine and emission control systems must be a California Air Resources Board (ARB) or U.S. Environmental Protection Agency (EPA) certified engine chassis configuration that meets or exceeds the requirements for the year and class of vehicle in which it is installed.

• A federally certified engine cannot be used in a vehicle that was originally certified for California.

• The installed engine and host chassis must retain all of their original emission control equipment. Diesel-to-gasoline conversions must have all gasoline engine and chassis emission control systems installed (such as fillpipe restrictor, catalytic converter and evaporative emission system).

• Don't mix engine and vehicle classifications. A heavy-duty engine cannot be installed in a light-duty exhaust-controlled chassis even if they have the same displacement. Non-emissions controlled powerplants such as industrial or off-road use-only engines may <u>not</u> be placed in any exhaust-controlled vehicle.

• No internal or external engine modifications (cams, pistons, intakes, etc.) may be performed unless the parts are ARB-exempted or EPA-certified for use in the installed engine.

• If a computer-controlled engine is to be installed in a non-computerized vehicle, the Check Engine Light and Assembly Line Data Link (ALDL) and all sensors, switches, wiring harnesses needed to make the system fully functional, must also be installed. The installation of the new engine must allow the testing of the ignition timing and the EGR system. Make sure the host vehicle's transmission is compatible with the new engine and computer system.

• These vehicles must pass a complete smog inspection (visual, functional, and tailpipe).

The preceding are guidelines for performing engine changes—they are not certification procedures. All exhaust emission controlled vehicles with engine changes must be inspected by an official referee station and must have a referee engine change label installed.

Remember, state and federal anti-tampering laws generally prohibit any modification to the vehicle's original emission control system configuration as certified by the manufacturer. In addition, Section 3362.1 of the California Code of Regulations prohibits any engine change that degrades the effectiveness of a vehicle's emission control system.

G-BODY ENGINE SWAP

1978-1987 Chevrolet El Caminos, Monte Carlos, Malibus, Buick Regals, Olds Cutlass, Pontiac Grand Prix, and Pontiac Lemans, are all built on the rear wheel drive G-Body chassis. These cars came with an assortment of engines and options. The G-Body chassis has excellent handling, excellent noise and vibration isolation, good brakes, a body-on-frame construction, great parts availability, etc. Due to the large number built, it will be the street machine of the '90s. We feel the G-body is a very underrated vehicle. We get to drive a number of different vehicles, and we often prefer the G-Body to Volvos, BMWs, even some Mercedes. The European cars often have better seats, but the G-Bodies (with the right options) are very comparable in terms of handling and braking, and the G-Body is superior in noise isolation, load capacity, suspension travel, and trailering capability. With the fuel-injected V8s and overdrive transmissions, the G-Bodies have better acceleration and fuel economy than the European cars. We really like the G-Bodies!

The G-Body TPI conversions would appear to be simple, straightforward conversions. However, like any engine swap, there are a lot of details that need to be addressed to successfully complete the conversion. This chapter will outline some of the important steps to ease the TPI/700-R4 conversion into the G-Bodies.

The TPI/TBI engines are virtual bolt-ins. If your vehicle did not originally have a Chevrolet small block, you will need to install the proper motor mounts to the front crossmember. The Camaro TPI/TBI engine brackets will work for the G-Body engine installation. The Firebird TPI engine works better for this swap than the Camaro TPI engine because the air cleaner ducting and battery cables fit this chassis with no modifications. The Camaro TPI air cleaner will not fit in the G-Body.

The 700-R4 transmission was never offered in the G-Body. The 700-R4 is longer than the Turbo-350, 200 and 200-4R transmissions that were offered in the G-Bodies. The driveshaft will need to be shortened 3 inches. To find a place that will shorten the driveshaft, look in the Yellow Pages under "Driveshaft." Shortening and balancing a driveshaft usually costs about $80.

On vehicles that came with the Turbo-350 and 200 transmissions (1978-1984), the transmission crossmember will need to be modified to install the 700-R4 transmission. On vehicles that came with the 200-4R transmission (1985-1988), a transmission tail housing from a 1982-1984 Caprice can be installed onto the 700-R4 transmission so that the transmission can be installed on to the 200-R4 crossmember. A 200-4R transmission crossmember cannot be bolted to G-Bodies that came with 3-speed automatic transmissions.

The shift linkage on all G-Bodies has enough travel to accommodate 4 forward gear positions.

On cars that did not originally have an ECM, the kick-panel from a newer model can be installed. The TPI/TBI ECM is bigger than the ECM used on some early computer controlled engines, so the kick-panel must be trimmed to allow installing the ECM.

The following pages show G-Bodies with TPI engines/700-R4 transmissions, and what was required to install them.

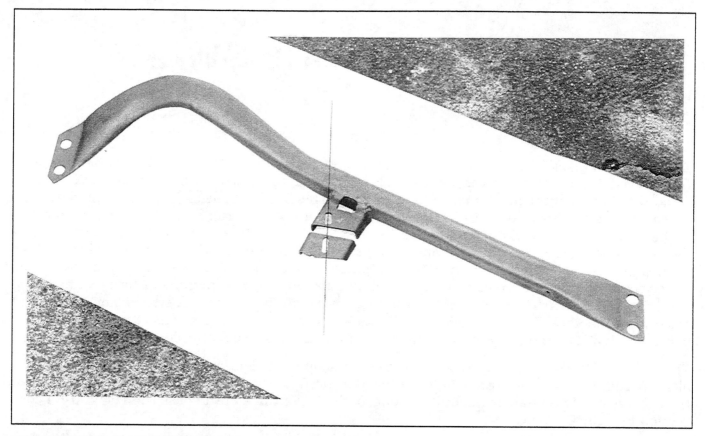

TRANSMISSION CROSSMEMBER

If your vehicle is equipped with the 200-4R transmission (1985-1988), the tailhousing from a 1982-1984 Caprice 700-R4 transmission must be used (see chapter on automatic transmissions).

On the 1978-1984 (non-200-4R transmission) G-Bodies, the transmission crossmember runs diagonally across the frame. The frame does not have provisions to relocate the crossmember rearward to accommodate the extra length of the 700-R4 transmission.

To use the existing crossmember, the front part of the perch must be cut off, and a slot cut into the remainder of the perch. Notice that the slot for the transmission mount is cut to follow the centerline of the transmission. Also, note the square clearance hole cut into the perch. The hole makes room for the left rear corner of the transmission mount.

Always test fit the transmission mount onto the crossmember to be sure there will be no metal to metal contact between the mount and the crossmember. There should be at least 3/8" all around the rubber mount to allow for normal engine movement.

If the transmissions is still too long for the crossmember, the crossmember can be bent very slightly by heating the crossmember tube with a torch, on the center line shown. Only bend the crossmember enough to accommodate the 700-R4 transmission. If any bending is required, it is very minimal. There should be no need to bend the crossmember more than 1/2", and in many cases, no bending is required.

If the crossmember is bent more than 1/2", the mounting holes may not align properly with the frame holes. If your vehicle has rubber isolators between the frame and the crossmember, do not enlarge the frame holes to correct for any misalignment because the isolators will not clamp properly.

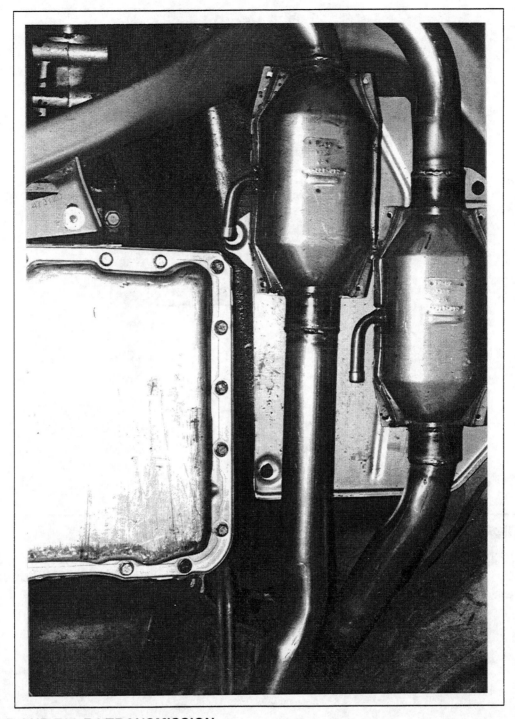

HEAT SHIELD AND 700-R4 TRANSMISSION

The stock G-Body heat shield over the catalytic converter will interfere with the 700-R4 transmission.

Note how the heat shield was trimmed to clear the transmission. Be sure to install the trimmed shield before you go to the muffler shop because it is very difficult to install the heat shield after the exhaust is in place.

The car is at the muffler shop for this photograph and the A.I.R. tubes to the catalytic converters have not yet been installed, but were installed after this photo was taken.

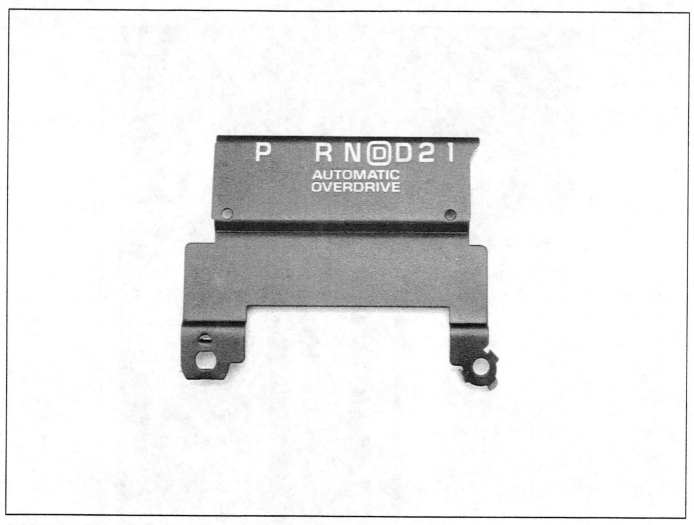

SHIFTER INDICATOR

On Malibus, El Caminos, and Monte Carlos, a gear selector plate for the overdrive transmission (part #25051915) provides the finishing touch to the 700-R4 transmission installation. The plate is a bolt-in and simply covers the original gear indicator label.

EXHAUST SYSTEM

This is the underside of a 1981 Malibu with a 1990 305 TPI/700-R4. The headpipe is from a 1987 V8 El Camino and is used with the "long" spacer (shown in the exhaust chapter). As mentioned in the exhaust chapter, some 1990-1992 305 TPI engines (such as the one shown above) use the same exhaust manifolds as the 305 TBI engines. The El Camino headpipe will not fit TPI engines with the large outlet exhaust manifolds. This headpipe is slightly restrictive for the 305 TPI engines, but it works well with the 305 TBI engines.

The 2-1/2" inlet catalytic converter is the same as that used for the 1990 TPI engines with the "TBI" manifolds. The exhaust hanger that bolts to the rear of the transmission and to the rear of the catalytic converter is from a 1991 Chevrolet Caprice. The stock Malibu heat shield (shown above the catalytic converter) was trimmed slightly to clear the 700-R4 transmission.

Note the modified crossmember, which accomodates the 700-R4 transmission.

MOUNTING THE RELAYS

On the G-Body, the TPI/TBI relays and bracketry cannot easily be mounted on the firewall because the windshield wiper linkage will be in the way. The relays cannot be mounted further rearward on the fender because the hood hinges and linkages will interfere.

The owner of this vehicle opted to extend the wires so the relays could be mounted on the fender, in a location where they will not interfere with anything. The windshield washer reservoir is not yet installed in this photo.

AIR CLEANER DUCTING, RADIATORS, AND RADIATOR SUPPORTS

This 1983 El Camino with a 1989 350 TPI is using 1985-1987 Firebird TPI air cleaner components. The flexible rubber duct to the throttle body is stretched slightly, but the components fit the G-Body very well. The air conditioning hoses had to be bent to clear the MAF sensor.

An electric cooling fan is normally required for this installation because of the remote air cleaner and ducting. The radiator support and electric cooling fan are from a Camaro/Firebird. A small section of the radiator support was cut out to clear the hood latch spring. Other than that, it was a bolt-in and will work with either the El Camino radiator, or the Camaro/Firebird TPI plastic-aluminum radiator.

If you are using the stock G-Body radiator, install a tee (available from Stealth Conversions, see chapter on cooling) into the lower radiator hose. The tee is a lot less expensive than modifying the radiator.

MORE AIR CLEANER DUCTING, RADIATORS, AND RADIATOR SUPPORTS

This is a 1981 Malibu with a 1990 305 TPI/700-R4.

The air cleaner ducting is from a 1990-1992 TPI Firebird. The 1988-1989 Firebird ducting and air cleaner looks similar, except for the MAF sensor. This ducting is easier to install into the G-Body than the 1985-1987 Firebird ducting shown on the previous page because it clears the air conditioner hoses better.

For cooling, a Flex-a-lite model 150 (Black Magic) electric cooling fan was installed in conjunction with a Camaro TPI plastic-aluminum radiator for maximum cooling with off the shelf parts. The Black Magic fan is offset to the driver's side to clear the air cleaner ducting, and a pusher fan (Flex-a-lite model 112) is mounted in front of the radiator, offset to the passenger's side. This combination offers good air distribution across the radiator and air conditioner condensor. The two fans combined are rated at nearly 3000 c.f.m. and draw nearly 28 amps. The TPI alternator is rated at 105 amps, so the current draw is not a problem. The air conditioning and fan pressure switch from the Firebird were installed on this car so that the electric cooling fans operate properly when the air conditioning is used.

While the electric fans are not as powerful as an engine-driven fan, the large and efficient radiator and the powerful electric cooling fans provide enough cooling capacity to allow mild towing in hot weather. For most applications, this set-up will be more than adequate.

The upper radiator hose is from a 1990 Corvette (the Camaro upper radiator hose was slightly short for this application) and the lower radiator hose is from a 1990 Camaro. The upper radiator support panel is made of metal and is from a 1987 Buick Grand National.

INDEX

INDEX

INDEX

SOURCE LIST

Edelbrock Corporation

throttle cable brackets & performance parts

2700 California St.
Torrance, CA 90503
(213) 781-2222

Flex-A-Lite

cooling system accessories

4540 South Adams
P.O. Box 9037
Tacoma, WA 98409
(206) 475-5772
(800) 851-1510 *Except in Washington State*
(800) 624-5646 *Washington State only*

Helm

factory service manuals

(800) 782-4356

K&N Engineering Inc.

air cleaners

P.O. Box 1329
Riverside CA 92502
(714) 684-9762

Lokar
throttle cables
10924 Murdock Dr.
Knoxville, TN 37922
(615) 966-2269

MSD Ignition

rev limiters

1490 Henry Brennan Dr.
El Paso, TX 79936
(915) 857-5200

NOS® Nitrous Oxide Systems
5930 Lakeside Drive.
Cypress, CA 90630
(714) 821-0580

Paxton Superchargers

air cleaner ducting

1260 Calle Suarte St.
Camarillo, CA 93012
(805) 987-5555

Red Line Synthetic Oil Corporation
3450 Pacheco Blvd.
Martinez, CA 94553
(510) 228-7576
(800) 624-7958

Stealth Conversions

vehicle speed sensors, air cleaner ducting

P.O. Box 11411
Pleasanton, CA 94588
FAX (510) 846-3642

Tilton Engineering

hydraulic clutch components

25 Easy St.
P.O. Box 1787
Buellton, CA 93427
(805) 688-2353
FAX (805) 688-2745

CHEVROLET TPI/TBI ENGINE SWAP MANUAL

Shows how to install the Chevrolet Tuned Port Injected and Throttle Body Injected Chevrolet V8s into older, non-fuel injected vehicles. Covers the electrical system (and how to use the factory wiring harness), fuel systems, air cleaner and ducting, overdrive transmissions, how to buy engines, smog laws, and much more! Over 180 pages, $24.00 (plus $3.00 for shipping and handling). California residents add 8.25% for sales tax.

CHEVROLET S-10 TRUCK V-8 CONVERSION MANUAL

Shows how to install a Chevrolet small block V8 into 2WD and 4X4 S-10 trucks and Blazers. Includes everything from drawings of the motor mounts to the detailed instructions and photographs for calibrating the factory tach to the V8. Over 150 pages, $29.00 (plus $3.00 for shipping and handling). California residents add 8.25% for sales tax.

DATSUN Z V8 CONVERSION MANUAL

Shows how to install a small block V8 into 1970-1978 Datsun Z cars. Covers everything from the drawings of the motor mounts to the detailed instructions on calibrating the tachometer. Also includes a chapter on suspension modifications to improve the handling of the V8 Z. Over 140 pages, $39.00 (plus $3.00 for shipping and handling). California residents add 8.25% for sales tax.

JAGUAR V8 CONVERSION MANUAL

Shows how to install a small-block V8 into 1972 through 1986 Jaguars. Covers everything from the drawings of the motor mounts to the detailed instructions on calibrating the tachometer. Also includes information to improve the ride of a V8 Jaguar. Over 120 pages, $35.00 (plus $3.00 for shipping and handling). California residents add 8.25% for sales tax.

Book Order Form (Circle Book(s) to be ordered)

Chevrolet TPI & TBI Engine Swapping	$24.00
Chevrolet S-10 Truck V8 Conversion Manual	$29.00
Datstun Z V8 Conversion Manual	$39.00
Jaguar V8 Conversion Manual	$34.95
Shipping. $3.00 per order (not per book)	$3.00
California residents, add 8.25% for sales tax	_____
C.O.D. Charge (if applicable)	$5.00
Second day air delivery available for C.O.D. orders for an additional $3.00.	_____
Total cost	_____

Ordering By C.O.D.

C.O.D. means Cash On Delivery. UPS will deliver the books, and you pay the UPS delivery person with a money order, check or cash. UPS charges $5.00 for the C.O.D. service. JTR does not do credit card orders at this time.

C.O.D.s are not possible to Canada.

For C.O.D. orders, call the order desk at (510)462-3619 from 9:30 a.m. to 4:30 p.m. Pacific Standard time, or use our FAX line at (510)846-3642 anytime. C.O.D. orders are normally shipped UPS ground service within two working days.

The order desk is an answering service and is not able to answer technical questions. Technical questions can be answered at (510)462-3619 from 5:00 p.m. to 6:30 p.m. on Tuesdays and Thursdays. Calls will be limited to 5 minutes, and C.O.D. orders can be placed.

Ordering by Mail.
Send Check or money order to:
JTR
P.O. Box 66
Livermore, CA 94551

Canadian residents, send US funds and add $3 for shipping.

Name _____

Address _____

City _____State_____ ZIP _____

Stealth Conversions Parts/Price list.
All Prices include shipping.

Stealth Conversions Parts/Price lists are to be used with JTR's *Chevrolet TPI & TBI Engine Swapping manual.* This insures that you know what you will be purchasing, and how the part(s) will be used. The very nature of engine swapping brings with it a lot of confusion, and questions that cannot be easily answered on the phone, therefore the *Chevrolet TPI & TBI Engine Swapping manual* will be necessary for you to order parts.

90° 3" i.d. Nitrile Rubber Elbow, 2.5" Centerline Radius, page 9-9	#3-90	$19
45° 3" i.d. Nitrile Rubber Elbow, 3.6" Centerline Radius, page 9-9	#3-45	$16
Radiator Hose Tee, page 13-12	#TEE	$12

Vehicle Speed Sensors

Note: All Stealth Conversions' Vehicle Speed Sensors do not require a buffer when used as described. All Vehicle Speed Sensors have a two year warrantee. All Veicle Speed Sensors are smog legal in California.

Two-Pulse. Use for all TBI and all computer controlled carbureted engines, and 1985-1989 TPI. Use for Truck ECMs requiring DRAC input. Comes with 10 feet of heavy-duty sheilded wire, page 12-5.

#2PHD $74

Four-Pulse. Use for 1990-1992 TPI and 1990-1992 Camaro Port Injected 3.1 V6 when not using 700-R4 transmission or Corvette ZF six-speed. Comes with 10 feet of heavy-duty sheilded wire, page 12-5.

#4PHD $89

Four-Pulse Integral Sleeve. For 1990-1992 TPI and 1990-1992 Camaro Port-Injected 3.1 V6 with 700-R4 transmission or Corvette ZF six-speed. Stock 1990-1992 TPI and 3.1 V6 wiring plugs directly into this unit. Unit comes with speedometer gear, Specify speedometer gear required (34-45 teeth), or list rear axle ratio, tire size, and color (blue, gray or red) of speedometer drive gear on the transmission output shaft, page 12-4.

#4PAC-(SPECIFY GEAR REQUIRED) Example, #4PAC-38 $65

Vehicle speed sensor signal conditioner module for trucks with electric speedometers using 1990-1992 TPI engines. This module is triggered by the electric speedometer signal, and conditions it for the 1990-1992 TPI ECM. Requires DRAC module used in late model trucks with anti-lock brakes, page 12-5.   #4PT $88

Vehicle speed sensor signal conditioner module for 1982-1987 Jaguars with electric speedometers using computer controlled carburreter, TBI or 1985-1989TPI, page 12-5   #2PJAG $85

Vehicle speed sensor signal conditioner module for 1982-1987 Jaguars with electric speedometers using 1990-1992 TPI engine, page 12-5.   #4PJAG $97

Stealth Conversions
Ordering by C.O.D.

C.O.D. means Cash On Delivery. UPS will deliver the parts, and you pay the UPS delivery person with a money order, cashier's check, or cash.

$30 minimum order an all C.O.D.s.

C.O.D.s are not possible to Canada.

For C.O.D. orders, call the order desk at (510)462-3619 from 9:30 a.m. to 4:30 p.m. Pacific Standard time, or use our FAX line at (510)846-3642 anytime. There is a $5 C.O.D. charge for orders under $150. Stealth Conversions' does not do credit card orders at this time.

The order desk is an answering service and is not able to answer technical questions. Technical questions can be answered at (510)462-3619 from 5:00 p.m. to 6:30 p.m. on Tuesdays and Thursdays. Calls will be limited to 5 minutes, and C.O.D. orders can be placed.

C.O.D. orders are normally shipped UPS ground service the following day. Please allow 8 working days for delivery to the east coast. Second Day air service is available for an additional $3 per item.

Ordering by mail.

Orders with cashier's checks or money orders are normally processed and shipped within five working days. Personal checks may be held two weeks. Parts are normally shipped UPS ground service. Please allow 12 working days for delivery to the east coast.

Please print clearly and leave a phone number so we can contact you if we have any questions about your order.

Send check or money order to:
Stealth Conversions
TPI/TBI Parts
P.O. Box 11411
Pleasanton, CA 94588

California residents, add 8.5% for sales tax.
Canadian residents, send US funds and add $5 for shipping.
Prices/specifications are subject to change without notice.